Edward Butts

Ed Butts is the author of several published books, most of them historical non-fiction. Many of his books are for adult readers, but he has also written for juveniles. Ed has had three books shortlisted for awards, including *The Desperate Ones*, nominated for an Arthur Ellis Award, and, most recently, *SOS: Stories of Survival*, nominated for a Red Maple Award. He is also the author of a humorous book about English grammar, *Idioms for Aliens*.

Ed has written hundreds of feature-length articles for various publications, including the *Globe and Mail, Toronto Star,* and *Old West Magazine*. His articles cover such topics as history, education, entertainment, humour, current events, travel, and writing. He has also written hundreds of short articles on a wide variety of topics — everything from gardening to airlines — for *www.ExquisiteWriting.com*. Ed lives in Guelph, Ontario.

In the same collection

Ven Begamudré, *Isaac Brock: Larger Than Life*
Lynne Bowen, *Robert Dunsmuir: Laird of the Mines*
Kate Braid, *Emily Carr: Rebel Artist*
Kathryn Bridge, *Phyllis Munday: Mountaineer*
William Chalmers, *George Mercer Dawson: Geologist, Scientist, Explorer*
Anne Cimon, *Susanna Moodie: Pioneer Author*
Deborah Cowley, *Lucille Teasdale: Doctor of Courage*
Gary Evans, *John Grierson: Trailblazer of Documentary Film*
Julie H. Ferguson, *James Douglas: Father of British Columbia*
Judith Fitzgerald, *Marshall McLuhan: Wise Guy*
lian goodall, *William Lyon Mackenzie King: Dreams and Shadows*
Tom Henighan, *Vilhjalmur Stefansson: Arctic Adventurer*
Stephen Eaton Hume, *Frederick Banting: Hero, Healer, Artist*
Naïm Kattan, *A.M. Klein: Poet and Prophet*
Betty Keller, *Pauline Johnson: First Aboriginal Voice of Canada*
Heather Kirk, *Mazo de la Roche: Rich and Famous Writer*
Vladimir Konieczny, *Glenn Gould: A Musical Force*
Michelle Labrèche-Larouche, *Emma Albani: International Star*
Wayne Larsen, *A.Y. Jackson: A Love for the Land*
Wayne Larsen, *James Wilson Morrice: Painter of Light and Shadow*
Francine Legaré, *Samuel de Champlain: Father of New France*
Margaret Macpherson, *Nellie McClung: Voice for the Voiceless*
Nicholas Maes, *Robertson Davies: Magician of Words*
Dave Margoshes, *Tommy Douglas: Building the New Society*
Marguerite Paulin, *René Lévesque: Charismatic Leader*
Marguerite Paulin, *Maurice Duplessis: Powerbroker, Politician*
Raymond Plante, *Jacques Plante: Behind the Mask*
Jim Poling Sr., *Tecumseh: Shooting Star, Crouching Panther*
T.F. Rigelhof, *George Grant: Redefining Canada*
Tom Shardlow, *David Thompson: A Trail by Stars*
Arthur Slade, *John Diefenbaker: An Appointment with Destiny*
Roderick Stewart, *Wilfrid Laurier: A Pledge for Canada*
Sharon Stewart, *Louis Riel: Firebrand*
André Vanasse, *Gabrielle Roy: A Passion for Writing*
John Wilson, *John Franklin: Traveller on Undiscovered Seas*
John Wilson, *Norman Bethune: A Life of Passionate Conviction*
Rachel Wyatt, *Agnes Macphail: Champion of the Underdog*

A QUEST BIOGRAPHY

HENRY HUDSON
NEW WORLD VOYAGER

EDWARD BUTTS

DUNDURN PRESS
TORONTO

Project Editor: Michael Carroll
Copy Editor: Cheryl Hawley
Designer: Jennifer Scott
Printer: Marquis

Library and Archives Canada Cataloguing in Publication

Butts, Edward, 1951-
    Henry Hudson : New World voyager / by Edward Butts.

Includes bibliographical references and index.
ISBN 978-1-55488-455-1

    1. Hudson, Henry, d. 1611. 2. Explorers--Great Britain--Biography. I. Title.

FC3211.1.H8B88 2009   910.92   C2009-902458-6

1   2   3   4   5   13   12   11   10   09

 Conseil des Arts du Canada   Canada Council for the Arts   Canada    ONTARIO ARTS COUNCIL CONSEIL DES ARTS DE L'ONTARIO

We acknowledge the support of the Canada Council for the Arts and the Ontario Arts Council for our publishing program. We also acknowledge the financial support of the Government of Canada through the Book Publishing Industry Development Program and The Association for the Export of Canadian Books, and the Government of Ontario through the Ontario Book Publishers Tax Credit program, and the Ontario Media Development Corporation.

Care has been taken to trace the ownership of copyright material used in this book. The author and the publisher welcome any information enabling them to rectify any references or credits in subsequent editions.

J. Kirk Howard, President

Printed and bound in Canada.
www.dundurn.com

Dundurn Press
3 Church Street, Suite 500
Toronto, Ontario, Canada
M5E 1M2

Gazelle Book Services Limited
White Cross Mills
High Town, Lancaster, England
LA1 4XS

Dundurn Press
2250 Military Road
Tonawanda, NY
U.S.A. 14150

Contents

Acknowledgements   9

Prologue: Adrift   11
Chapter 1: Out of Obscurity   15
Chapter 2: Over the North Pole   24
Chapter 3: To Novaya Zemlya   49
Chapter 4: Dutch Intrigues   75
Chapter 5: Secrets and a Sacred Oath   99
Chapter 6: The Voyage of the *Half Moon*   111
Chapter 7: Arrest and Reprieve   149
Chapter 8: Beyond the Furious Overfall   164
Chapter 9: Mutiny   180
Epilogue   188

Chronology of Henry Hudson   191
Bibliography   201
Index   202

To the Butts family of Florence, Cape Breton, Nova Scotia, which has had its share of mariners and adventurers.

Acknowledgements

My thanks to Michael Carroll and Kirk Howard of Dundurn for offering me this wonderful project and to Cheryl Hawley for her editorial contributions. I also owe thanks to Library and Archives Canada and the Guelph, Ontario, Public Library. An excellent online account of Henry Hudson's career can be found at *www.ianchadwick.com/hudson.*

I am indebted to all the elementary school teachers and high school history teachers who first introduced me to heroes like Henry Hudson. They instilled in me a love of history, Canadian and otherwise, that I have never lost.

Prologue

Adrift

Captain Henry Hudson sits in the stern of the shallop, his face a solemn mask. Should any of the others in the boat steal a glance at him, he does not wish them to see hopeless despair in his eyes; so he keeps his gaze on the wall of mist that lies across the green water like a distant low cloud. It is as though he believes that by staring long and hard enough, his eyes might pierce that fog to see what lies beyond. He has one hand on the tiller, and all of his concentration seems to be on navigating the open boat that is now their world. But behind that determined countenance, a thousand thoughts are tossing like ships on a stormy sea. *Is this the end? How did everything come to this? What to do next? If only I had seen it coming! If … if … if….*

Young John Hudson lies propped against his father's legs, his head on his father's lap. He is nineteen years old. No longer a boy, but not quite a man. The lad is quiet. But the captain has a hand on John's shoulder, and he can feel him shivering. Is that from the cold, the captain wonders, or is it out of fear? *Does my son wonder if he'll ever see his mother again?* The captain thinks of his wife Katherine back in their comfortable home in London. Will he somehow find a way to take John back to her, alive and well? If, God forbid, he cannot, will she forgive him for taking John on this voyage, or will she curse her husband's name for the rest of her days? If only he could see her one more time! And his other two sons! And his baby grandchild! The captain squeezes John's shoulder as he steers the shallop around yet another ice floe. *The wretches could at least have spared the lad!* But of course, he knows very well why the mutineers could not risk taking John back to England. His testimony would hang them all!

Henry Hudson knows that his teenaged son has every reason to be afraid on this June day in 1611. The two Hudsons and seven crewmen from the ship *Discovery* are adrift in a small boat on a cold northern sea. Three of the men are ill, and two are suffering from injuries. They are in unknown territory, so far from home they might as well be on the moon. Their provisions are puny: a gun with a little shot and powder, a small bag of flour, a few blankets, some pikes, an iron cooking pot, a box of carpenter's tools, and the clothes on their backs. That is all they have to help them survive in a hostile Arctic environment.

Mutiny! Of all the crimes men of the sea could stoop to, none is more despicable in the eyes of God and man. Hudson has faced the vile spectre of mutiny before, and always he has managed to circumvent it, by means of reason, by compromise ... until now! This time the mutineers struck so swiftly, there had been no opportunity to negotiate. They had not even the desire to listen. This mutiny was not only an act to depose the captain;

it was also a culling of the weakest members of the crew so there would be fewer men eating the dwindling supply of food.

Ever since conquering the Furious Overfall a year ago, a feat accomplished by no other mariner before him, Hudson has been certain that he has reached the Pacific Ocean — or at least an extension of it. *The way to China and the Indies was almost within my grasp. If only the men could have understood that! We would all have returned to England as heroes and reaped rewards and glory.*

Hudson examines their options. They can follow the *Discovery*, and perhaps catch up with the ship at the place where they had found a breeding ground for sea birds months earlier. He knows the mutineers will stop there to stock up on as many birds as they can. But will they stay long enough?

Hudson thinks of navigating the shallop through the Furious Overfall. Then they could travel south, hugging the Labrador coast until they reach Newfoundland. If they get there they could go home with the fishing fleet. But Hudson realizes that is a long, long way to go in an open boat. And they have so little food.

Hundreds of miles to the south, the French have established a settlement in the valley of the St. Lawrence River. Hudson wonders if he they could make it there overland, perhaps with the help of the Natives. The French and the English are not on friendly terms, but surely those French would show Christian charity to a handful of unfortunate Englishmen. *But would the savages help us, or kill us?*

The other option is to find a spot somewhere on the bleak shore of this northern sea and await rescue. If the mutineers reach England, Hudson believes, no doubt they will have a grand lie prepared to explain how the captain and so many men were lost. But somebody will be suspicious, and the truth will come out. Then an expedition will be sent to look for them. Even if the *Discovery* does not return to England, an expedition will still be sent. People will want to know what happened to the ship and crew. Others will want to take up the quest for the Northwest Passage. Two or three years might pass, but eventually another English ship will find its way through the Furious Overfall and into this sea. Hudson is positive of that.

If we reach land, we can build a good sturdy shelter. If we can shoot one of those great, white bears, we will have meat. If we can convince the savages to help us; promise them rewards … if … if … if….

Looking ahead, Hudson sees the fog bank rolling toward them. It crosses the cold, green water like a grey shroud. There is no escaping it. The mist envelopes the little boat and its doomed passengers, and the fate of Henry Hudson and his men becomes an Arctic mystery.

1

Out of Obscurity

For a man who was the foremost northern navigator of his time, surprisingly little is known about Henry Hudson's life before he made his first important voyage in 1607. No record of his birth has ever been found, but it has been estimated that he was probably born about 1570. That would make him thirty-seven, considered middle age in that era, by the time he first burst upon the historical stage. He and his wife Katherine had three sons: Oliver, John, and Richard, who was still a small boy at the time of Hudson's disappearance. The family lived in a narrow, three-storey brick house in the suburb of St. Katherine, near the Tower of London. This was a fairly respectable neighbourhood, so while Hudson was not rich, he evidently had a comfortable income. He could even afford to pay for a maidservant to help Katherine with the daily chores. Today the Hudson family would be considered upper middle class.

Nothing is known of Hudson's parents, but one of the founders of the Muscovy Company, an important trading firm, was Henry Heardson, who *might* have been Hudson's grandfather. If so, that would help explain Hudson's association with that company. Henry Heardson was also an alderman; a member of the London municipal government. This suggests that the family had political connections. Another founder of the Muscovy Company was Sebastian Cabot, son of the explorer John Cabot, who had discovered Newfoundland and its rich fishing grounds for England. Sebastian Cabot had searched for the Northwest Passage, and no doubt talked to Henry Heardson about finding a short route to China. A Christopher Hudson, who might have been Henry's older brother, had been an agent for the Muscovy Company. A Thomas Hudson, who also might also have been an older brother, had been a sea captain for the Muscovy Company. At a time when Henry would have been in his mid-teens, Thomas met the explorer John Davis.

Though no details are known, Henry Hudson was well educated. He could read and write, do mathematics, and had a passion for books about exotic places. He knew how to use a quadrant to determine a ship's position by the stars. It is quite possible that young Hudson sailed with John Davis in 1587, when Davis encountered what he called the Furious Overfall, while searching for the Northwest Passage. This body of water, with its powerful currents and ice floes that were so dangerous to wooden sailing ships, is now called Hudson Strait. After that voyage, Hudson almost certainly served aboard an English ship in the battle with the Spanish Armada in 1588.

By 1607 Hudson was a licensed pilot and ship's captain, which meant he had to have had considerable experience at sea. He could have sailed merchant ships in the Atlantic and the Mediterranean Sea. He might even have engaged in a little piracy. It was not at all uncommon for merchant sailors to turn to robbery on the high seas if an opportunity presented itself, and the ships of rival countries were always considered fair game. The depredations of English pirates were the main reason the king of Spain had sent the Armada to attack England.

While there is no solid evidence that Hudson explored with Davis, sailed as a merchant mariner or a pirate, or fought the Spanish Armada, none of these things would have been out of character for him. What is known for sure from surviving records is that he was a man who craved adventure. Hudson was at home on the deck of a ship. He was a driven man, with no fear of the unknown. If he had, in fact, seen the Furious Overfall while sailing with Davis, the idea of finding the Northwest Passage could have taken root in his mind then. Whatever its source, that idea became Hudson's lifelong obsession.

No authenticated portrait of Henry Hudson is known to exist. All of the pictures alleged to be likenesses of him were made after his death, and come from the artists' imaginations. A verbal description of Hudson written by a man who knew him says he was fair-haired and thin.

Accounts from his contemporaries portray Hudson as a good husband and father, but a moody man with a sharp temper. He was shy socially and he shunned public adulation. His friends included such notable individuals as Captain John Smith, the founder of the Jamestown Colony in Virginia; Sir Thomas Smythe, one of England's greatest merchant adventurers; and Richard Hakluyt, the famous author and geographer. Hakluyt was a strong believer in exploration and colonization, and counted among his friends most of the renowned English sea

This is believed to be a likeness of Henry Hudson. However, all alleged portraits of Hudson were made after his death, so the authenticity of the image is uncertain.

Library and Archives Canada C-017727.

captains of his time, including Sir Francis Drake. Smith, Smythe, and Hakluyt always spoke highly of Henry Hudson.

Hudson was a straightforward man who wanted one thing: to sail a ship on voyages of discovery. For that he was better equipped intellectually and evidently had more experience than the average English sea captain. Hudson did, however, have failings; he was a poor judge of character, and he was not a good leader of men. These shortcomings would blight his career as an explorer, and ultimately bring about his destruction.

The driving force behind the Age of Exploration was profit. While men like Henry Hudson were always willing to venture into new territory to see what lay beyond the horizon, the fact remained that expeditions of discovery were expensive. Ships had to be purchased and provisioned. Sailors had to be paid. Money-conscious monarchs, always short of cash because of wars and extravagant lifestyles, were not willing to invest in expeditions unless they were guaranteed some sort of financial return. The great trading enterprises like the Muscovy Company and the East India Company of England were run by hard-headed businessmen who measured everything, including their own lives, in terms of pounds, shillings, and pence. They sponsored explorers not for the sheer sake of expanding knowledge, but to fill their own coffers.

There was a great demand in Europe for products from the Far East: Exotic goods, such as spices and silks. Spices that improved the flavour of poorly preserved food, particularly meat. Garments, bedding, and various accessories made of silk became a fashion rage in Europe. A nobleman of the aristocracy or a gentleman of the growing urban middle class wanted a full wardrobe of silk garments, from his socks and underwear to his brightly coloured outer coat. The lady he escorted to a dinner party or the theatre simply had to be dressed in a fashionable silk gown. And no lady or gentleman was considered properly dressed without a scented silk handkerchief tucked into a bodice, sleeve, or pocket.

Because these commodities had to be transported incredibly long distances, they were very expensive. Caravans from the Orient carried the goods overland to the eastern Mediterranean, where they were sold at top prices. There, powerful Italian city states, such as Venice, had an iron grip on trade. They purchased the spices, silks, and other Eastern goods, and then added their own high mark up before selling the products to the rest of Europe. Thus, by the time an ounce of pepper or cinnamon, or a bolt of silk reached London, it was literally worth its weight in gold.

The monopoly the Italians had on trade with the Far East was not the only problem for the nations of Western Europe. Muslim armies had overrun North Africa and even much of Eastern Europe. Now the ships of Muslim pirates like the Barbary Corsairs and the Salee Rovers prowled the Mediterranean, preying on European shipping. These pirates wanted not only the cargoes the ships were carrying, but also the crewmen. White Europeans fetched good prices in the slave markets of North Africa.

The maritime nations of Western Europe began looking for other routes to the Far East. Portuguese navigators pioneered a shipping lane down around the African continent and into the Indian Ocean. This route was also very long — a round trip could take two years — and it was infested with pirates. The Portuguese government negotiated treaties with the various rulers to whom many of the pirates were subject, and gained safe passage for Portuguese ships. But the vessels of other European countries were not granted this protection, which suited the Portuguese.

When the Italian navigator Christopher Columbus, sailing for Spain, made his first monumental voyage in 1492, he was not looking for new lands. He was trying to prove that a ship could sail directly from Europe all the way to the Far East. When he landed at an island in what are now called the West Indies, he actually thought he was near India. Further exploration by Columbus and other mariners sailing for Spain and Portugal revealed that he had stumbled upon a "New World" that would eventually be called America. Spain and Portugal claimed the new lands for themselves and established colonial empires.

Meanwhile, the merchants of Western Europe still desperately wanted a new sea route to the Far East. They thought that America was just an island that their ships could sail around. But with each voyage of discovery the "island" kept getting bigger as more miles of coastline were added to the maps. Finally, a Portuguese explorer named Ferdinand Magellan, sailing for Spain, found the way around the southern tip of South America. Now a ship could actually sail from Europe to the Far East, via the Atlantic and Pacific oceans. But this route was still incredibly long and full of dangers. One of the worst hazards was scurvy, a disease caused by a vitamin-poor diet that plagued sailors on long voyages.

With Spain and Portugal jealously guarding the sea lanes of the South Atlantic, the French and the English began to search for a more northerly route through or around America — a Northwest Passage. They concluded that because the circumference of the Earth is smaller at the higher latitudes, the Northwest Passage would be the major link in a short, commercially viable trade route to the Far East. Moreover, the country that found and controlled the passage would not only profit from trade, but would have a major card to play in political dealings with other European countries.

French and English expeditions probed the east coasts of what are now Canada and the United States, looking for a way through a land mass whose size they did not know. The French explorer Jacques Cartier sailed up the St. Lawrence River, hoping it would lead him to the Pacific Ocean. He was disappointed, though his discoveries marked the beginning of a French empire in North America. John Cabot, an Italian sailing for England, was the first to add Newfoundland to English charts. Explorers who came after him, like Martin Frobisher and John Davis, made the initial attempts to unravel the riddles of the Arctic Ocean.

Sir Martin Frobisher followed in Hudson's footsteps, discovering Frobisher Bay in Baffin Island, as well as a large amount of pyrite (fool's gold).

Frobisher's story illustrates how little Europeans knew of the Far North. When he sailed into an inlet of Baffin Island (Frobisher Bay), he thought he was in a channel that separated the continents of Asia and America. Frobisher's exploration was sidetracked when he returned to England with a rock that assayers were convinced contained gold. The result was Canada's first gold rush. Investors, including Queen Elizabeth I, sent Frobisher back as the leader of a major expedition to mine gold. It turned out that Frobisher had found worthless fool's gold. The Queen of England lost a lot of money in the venture — an example of why monarchs were hesitant to invest in voyages — and Martin Frobisher's career as an explorer was over.

However, Frobisher saw the Furious Overfall. He wanted to explore it, but could not because he had been ordered to mine gold. Years later John Davis, and maybe a youthful Henry Hudson, also saw that turbulent strait. Pans of ice that came barrelling down the Overfall like battering rams forced Davis to turn back. For a man like Hudson, the Furious Overfall was a challenge to be taken up with daring. If only he could get a chance at it!

2

Over the North Pole

One January day in 1607, the gentlemen of the Muscovy Company held a meeting in their office on a street called Budge Row. It was a short, unimpressive looking street, but it was the centre of London's wholesale marketplace. The merchants of Budge Row did business with the world. For the Muscovy Company, as indeed for all of the company's merchant rivals, the world presented some complex geographical problems.

Ever since the English defeat of the Spanish Armada in 1588, England had grown from a second-rate, backwater country to a major military power and trading nation. Skeptics said that it was the weather more than anything else that had destroyed the Armada, but every good Englishman knew it had been the skill of English captains and the accuracy of the English gunners that had saved the country from the mightiest invasion fleet ever assembled. The humbling of Spain, the most powerful nation in Europe, had brought the English respect, prestige, and confidence. English commerce grew as merchants aggressively sought new markets. Every year saw more and more ships in the Pool, London's main anchorage in the River Thames. Across the sea the Dutch, whose country had long lain under Spanish domination, had been encouraged to rebel. With English help, they had thrown off the Spanish yoke. Now Dutch merchants were rivals of the English and had even managed to establish their own trade route around Africa, sending Dutch ships into waters that had once been the private highways of the Portuguese.

The men of the Muscovy Company knew that in the ever-shifting world of commerce two things were essential to the survival of an enterprise: growth and adaptability. Their company was so-named because it traded with Russia, and had factors (agents) in Moscow. From Russia the company imported furs, tallow (used to make soap and candles), wax, hemp, flax, and timber. The Muscovy Company's main export to Russia was cloth. English cloth was considered the best in the world, and the Russians used it to make coats and other clothing that could stand up to the brutal Russian winter.

Muscovy Company ships sailed north from England, around the top of Norway, then down to the White Sea and the Russian port of Arkhangel'sk. For years the English had had this trade route to themselves, but now the Dutch were also sending merchant vessels to Arkhangel'sk. That worried the men of the Muscovy Company. What's more, their spies in Amsterdam had told them that the Dutch were planning to search for a Northeast Passage.

The idea of a Northeast Passage, as opposed to a Northwest Passage, was nothing new. About eighty years earlier an Englishman named Robert Thorne had tried to convince King

Henry VIII to finance a voyage to the Far East by way of the North Pole. People of that day thought that all of the ice floating in the northern ocean came from rivers that flowed into the sea at high latitudes. They held this belief because the water from a piece of melted sea ice was always fresh. They did not realize that when seawater freezes, the salt leeches out of the ice and back into the sea. They knew that some ice could form along coastlines in the winter, but they did not believe it was possible for ice to form in large bodies of salt water.

Thorne reasoned that in the summer, when there were weeks of constant daylight in the high Arctic, the sun's rays would melt the ice and leave the sea open for navigation. He proposed a northern voyage to prove it. King Henry would not sponsor such a voyage, so Thorne had his theory published in a pamphlet called "Thorne's Plan". In it he said, "There is no land uninhabitable or sea innavigable." Then he went on to explain his Plan. "Now then, if from Newfoundland the sea be navigable, there is no doubt, but sailing Northward and passing the Pole, descending to the Equinoctical line, we shall arrive at the islands of Cathay, and it should be a much shorter way than any other."

Over the years Thorne's theory had been discussed and enhanced by some of the religious thought peculiar to the time. Christians believed that the North Pole was located on an island. Because of its geographic importance, they reasoned, God would make the North Pole's location a place of great beauty and dignity. To many people it just seemed to make sense that God, in his wisdom, would protect the North Pole from Arctic ice.

The men of the Muscovy Company did not place much belief in such far-fetched tales as God planting a little paradise in the midst of the Arctic waste. However, nobody had ever put

Robert Thorne's seemingly rational theory to the test. Now they wanted to do just that.

If there was indeed an ocean at the top of the world that was ice free during the summer, all that was needed was for someone to find a way through the pack ice that apparently surrounded it. The explorer could then sail past the North Pole on temperate waters, breach the icefields again at a more easterly location, and then continue south to China and Japan. But who was the man to lead such an expedition? That was what the men of the Muscovy Company had gathered to discuss.

Money was of principal importance to these men. They did not want to spend any more than was absolutely necessary. They had already approached King James I for financial support. The king had given their endeavour his royal blessing, but he would not contribute a penny. The Muscovy merchants therefore wanted a competent leader, but one who would not charge too much for his services.

Captain John Smith's name came up during the meeting. But it was pointed out that the famous adventurer had already been engaged to take colonists to Virginia. Then someone suggested Henry Hudson. According to the minutes of that meeting, one of the Muscovy merchants said of Hudson, "He is an experienced sea pilot, and he has in his possession secret information that will enable him to find the north-east passage."

That sounded like a good recommendation, but these hard-nosed businessmen wanted solid references. The Muscovy Company sent a deputation to the port city of Bristol to talk to the man who knew more about sea captains and exploration than anyone else in England, Richard Hakluyt.

The scholar who greeted the Muscovy Company delegation in his private study was one of the great Englishmen of his time. He had been Secretary of State for the late Queen Elizabeth I and for her successor King James. He was one of the driving forces behind the colonization of Virginia. He was an ordained priest who had held important positions at Bristol Cathedral and Westminster Abbey. But most importantly for these visitors, Hakluyt was well acquainted with scores of ship's masters. That this great man had a passion for the sea and for exploration was evident. His study was piled high with books and pamphlets on the subject. Nautical charts covered the tables, hung on the walls, or stood in rolls in a tall vase, like so many walking sticks. Hakluyt's opinion of Henry Hudson would carry a lot of weight.

The Muscovy men got right to the point. They told Hakluyt about their planned polar expedition and asked if he would recommend Henry Hudson to lead it. Hakluyt replied without hesitation, "Henry Hudson is the most qualified man in England for your venture."

There was no putting it anymore clearly than that. Then one of the Muscovy Company delegates asked, in an almost conspiratorial tone, "Is it true that Captain Hudson knows of a secret route to Cathay?"

Hakluyt's only response was a knowing smile. Did Hudson know of a secret route to Cathay, as many people then called China? It was foolish of the man to even ask the question. Nobody gave away important secrets concerning exploration or commerce. Spies were everywhere. Everybody was looking for the advantages to be gained by privileged information. Merchants wanted first crack at profitable sources, markets, and trade routes. Monarchs needed new revenues that would increase their power and prestige. Mariners like Hudson competed for expeditions for which they would be paid, and perhaps even gain glory.

Not long after their interview with Richard Hakluyt, the directors of the Muscovy Company invited Henry Hudson to an interview. His house was not far from their office, so the captain would have walked through the busy, grimy streets of London. Because it was January, the stench of rotting garbage, animal droppings, and human waste would not have been as pungent as it was in the warmer months. Hudson would have worn a hooded woolen cloak to keep out the cold. Beneath that, for this occasion, he would have been dressed like the respectable Elizabethan gentleman he was. Good Queen Bess had been dead not quite four years, but the fashions of her reign were still very much in vogue. Hudson would have worn a pullover shirt with billowy sleeves, under a close-fitting, sleeveless vest called a jerkin, puffy breeches, and silk stockings. Since this was not a strictly formal occasion, he probably did not bother with the wide, frilly Elizabethan collar that required a hundred or so pins to keep in place. Because of the time of year he would have worn long boots, rather than fashionable buckle shoes. Hudson would have carried a stout walking stick; not that he needed one to help him along, but to discourage criminals. The streets of London were crawling with pickpockets, cutpurses, and footpads — the seventeenth century term for a mugger.

Quite likely Hudson already knew why he had been summoned to the Muscovy Company's office. His friend Richard Hakluyt would undoubtedly have written to him about his meeting with the deputation. Hudson would have been thrilled to be given a chance to look for the Northeast Passage, though he had doubts such a route existed. But this could be an opportunity for him to look for the Northwest Passage. The "secret route to Cathay" that the Muscovy merchant had asked Hakluyt about was, in fact, the Northwest Passage. Hudson did not know exactly where it was, though rumour claimed he did, but he

An engraving of Henry Hudson receiving his commission from the Muscovy Company.

was sure he had a good idea of where to look. Shortly after his interview with the Muscovy merchants, Hudson revealed his thoughts when he wrote to tell Hakluyt he had agreed to command the expedition.

> I take leave of England in a few months to test the theory that a route to Cathay can be found across the half-frozen seas that cover the roof of the world. I shall come to you at Bristol, and with your permission shall study your charts of that region.
>
> The hopes of my employers are higher than mine that this venture will succeed. I fear the ice may prove too thick. But we shall persevere.

If the route be not found to the north, I know
another. Would there were at [my] disposal
all that others have gleaned about my Furious
Overfall in the western sea. There, I know, lies
the sure sea path to the Indies, and he who finds
it will be remembered for all time, even as Drake
will not be forgot. I pray with all my heart. Be it
by northern path or western, I would that my
name be carved on the tablets of the sea.

Hudson spent some time in Bristol with Hakluyt, discussing the expedition and studying all the charts and documen-
tation available on the northern seas. Much of what had been
written was pure speculation and even outright fantasy. Charts
showed islands that did not exist, or failed to show islands that
did. Hakluyt showed Hudson a letter in which another would-be
geographer, the Reverend Samuel Purchas, commented on how
simple it would be to sail over the top of the world to China. "If
either by North-east or North-west or North a passage be open,
the sight of the globe easily sheweth with how much ease, in how
little time and expense the same might be affected…."

When Hudson returned to London he found Katherine in
an unhappy mood. She was accustomed to her husband being
away from home for long periods of time. That was part of
being a mariner's wife. She had not objected when Hudson
said he would be taking their son John along as ship's boy. The
lad wanted to go to sea, and who better to teach him the mariner's trade than his own father? What annoyed Katherine was
the rather small sum of one hundred pounds that Hudson had
agreed to accept for his services. She thought he should have
asked for more money. Though Hudson had a verbal agreement

with the Muscovy Company, he had not yet signed a contract. Katherine put her foot down and told Hudson that for the sake of his family, he had better demand better payment.

Hudson was embarrassed to haggle over money, but he knew Katherine was right. He was so happy to have this expedition, he'd probably have gone for nothing. But he was also aware that the company was underpaying him for a voyage that would be hazardous, but could ultimately prove very profitable for them. When Hudson demanded more money, the Muscovy men wrung their hands and wailed about piratical sea captains. They finally, reluctantly, agreed to pay Hudson an additional thirty pounds and five shillings.

Hudson would be making his voyage in a Muscovy Company ship called the *Hopewell*. Like most of the merchant vessels of the time, the *Hopewell* was a bark; a small, square-rigged ship of about eighty tons with two principal masts and a short foremast. She was made of seasoned oak. The *Hopewell* had already made two trips to the cold Baltic Sea, and four down the Atlantic coast to Portugal, so she was known to be seaworthy. The steering wheel so often associated with sailing ships had not yet been developed in Hudson's time. All ships were steered by means of a whipstaff, a bar attached to the tiller.

Though the *Hopewell* was only three years old, and Hudson had her seams sealed with gum, like all wooden sailing ships she leaked. Hand operated pumps were used to get water out of the hold, but there would always be some bilge water sloshing around in the bottom. Also, like every other ship afloat, the *Hopewell* had rats. Most ships had a cat aboard not as a pet or a mascot, but to keep the rat population down. To completely clear a ship of rats would have been next to impossible, because every port a ship visited was infested with them. Rats got aboard simply by scurrying along the ropes that secured a ship to a wharf.

Hudson would have personally seen to the provisioning of the ship. Into the hold went the main food supplies: pickled beef and pork, dried beef, dried peas, cheese, hardtack biscuits, and barley meal. Fresh fruit and vegetables like apples, carrots, and onions would be consumed early during the voyage, before they had a chance to spoil. As captain, Hudson would take aboard his own food supplies, which might include such luxuries as butter. They were stored in his private larder and cooked separately from the crew's meals. The captain also had his own galley, with the stove set in a box of sand to prevent fire. The ship's casks would be filled with fresh water. There would also be a supply of beer, and the captain would have a stock of wine for his personal use.

Among the many items loaded into the *Hopewell*'s hold were several barrels of salt for preserving fish. When crewmen were not busy with shipboard duties, they would spend some of their off-time fishing. The fish they caught would be cleaned and salted down for when the *Hopewell* returned to England. The Muscovy Company would then sell the fish to help defray the cost of the expedition.

Hiring a crew for the voyage would not have been difficult. London was a commercial maritime centre, and there were always sailors looking for work. Some of those who made up the *Hopewell*'s crew might very well have sailed with Hudson previously. Little is known about them except their names, but no doubt they were experienced seamen. First mate was William Collin, who had his master's license and so was qualified to be a captain. James Young was the bos'un (boatswain), a ship's junior officer. The other crewmen were John Colman, John Cooke, James

Beuberry, James Skrutton, John Playse, Thomas Baxter, Richard Day, and James Knight. Young John Hudson was aboard as the ship's boy. As the captain's son, John Hudson would be entitled to the respect of the common sailors, but he had no authority. He did not share his father's cabin or table, but slept and ate with the men. Besides Hudson, only the first mate had his own cabin. The rest of the men slept in the crew's cramped quarters below decks.

On April 19, 1607, a special service was held for the ship's company in tiny St. Ethelburga's Church on Bishopsgate Street in London. Crowded into the smallest church in the city were Hudson, Katherine, his crewmen and the wives of any who were married, the directors of the Muscovy Company, and all of their servants. The clergyman delivered a sermon titled "God's Known Realm," and offered up prayers for the safe return of the ship and men. Hudson and the crew took Communion. They expected to weigh anchor in four days.

In spite of the prayers for fair weather, the elements did not cooperate. For two weeks unusually thick fog, followed by a storm with gale-force winds, kept the *Hopewell* in harbour at Gravesend, twenty-six miles downriver from London. This was not a good beginning, because in the short navigation season of the Far North every day counted. Finally, on May 1, the *Hopewell* sailed from Gravesend.

Contrary winds made the going slow. Twenty-six days after setting sail, Hudson was eighteen miles east of the Shetland Islands off northern Scotland. Over the next four days he covered only ninety miles. Another week passed before he crossed the Arctic Circle.

Life aboard ship was one of routine and monotony when seas were calm, and great danger when they weren't. Every man had a duty to perform, from menial tasks like swabbing the

New World Voyager

decks, to the more hazardous job of climbing up to the yard-arms to furl or unfurl sails. Orders came from the captain or the mate to the bo'sun or the bo'sun's mate, who passed them on to the crew. The safety of the ship depended upon every man doing his job promptly and efficiently.

Almost all common seamen came from the lower class. In general, sailors were illiterate and superstitious. No matter how tough a sailor was, like all working class people he learned at a very young age to be submissive to authority and humble in the presence of people considered to be his social superiors.

Sailors on privately owned vessels were not necessarily subjected to the brutal discipline that existed on naval ships. Nonetheless, aboard any ship the captain was the law and his authority was not to be questioned. A captain had the right to promote men or demote them, and with demotion came a reduction in pay. If a sailor failed to do his job properly or was insubordinate, the captain could mildly reprimand him, or subject him to harsh punishment.

With men living together in close quarters for extended periods of time, it was inevitable that disputes and quarrels would break out. Some captains kept such situations in check by running a "tight ship." That meant the captain would tolerate no slacking, no squabbling, and no trouble. Troublemakers were punished. However, the captain had to be consistent in his dispensation of punishments and rewards. To be inconsistent could be taken as a sign of weakness. A captain also had to avoid showing favouritism, as that could breed jealousy and trouble.

At some point early on this voyage something must have happened to cause Hudson to be unhappy with the performance of his ship's officers. He did not record any details in his log, but there was a sudden flurry of promotion and demotion. William

Collin was demoted from mate to bo'sun. This would have been humiliating to a man who had his master's license. The former bos'un, James Young, was demoted to common seaman. Mariner John Colman was given the rank of mate. This was a major shift in the hierarchy of such a small company of men, and in a severely restricted environment in which there were so many potential threats to harmony.

A wooden sailing ship was not a comfortable place for the common sailor. The work was hard and often dangerous. There were scores of different ways a man could be killed or seriously injured. Merchant ships did not usually carry doctors. If a man was injured, the ship's carpenter might do duty as a surgeon. He had the tools for splinting a broken bone, hacking off a shattered or infected arm or leg, or pulling out an aching tooth. The part of the ship below decks where sailors worked, slept, and ate was cramped, damp, and gloomy. It smelled of tar, bilgewater, rotting food, and unwashed men, clothing, and bedding. There was no toilet on the ship. The men urinated over the side, or they went to a location at the bow of the ship called the "seat of easement" through which bodily wastes dropped into the sea.

Meals were often a daily fare of porridge, salt meat, hardtack biscuits, and cheese. On long voyages, the fresh water in the barrels would go scummy, and the biscuits would get wormy. The sailors received a daily ration of beer, but drunkenness was not allowed. After weeks at sea, the beer might turn sour.

By the end of May, Hudson found that his compass behaved erratically. "This day I found the needle to incline seventy-nine degrees under the horizon," he recorded in his log. Hudson was no doubt mystified by this. Navigators in his time did not realize that the farther above the Arctic Circle they sailed, the less reliable the compass became. They had little understanding of the relationship between the Magnetic North Pole and the Geographic North Pole. Some navigators were not even aware of the difference between the two poles, let alone the fact that the Magnetic Pole drifts from place to place.

This made it very difficult for a northern explorer like Hudson to plot a course or determine his exact location. In more southerly positions, Hudson could easily determine latitude by the sun or stars. But in the Arctic, atmospheric distortions resulted in errors. What's more, nobody had yet come up with a reliable method for determining longitude. For that, navigators had to use "dead reckoning," a system based on the ship's speed, the course steered, and the last observation of latitude. A ship's speed could only be roughly estimated by tossing a marker over the side and measuring the time it took for the ship to sail past it. All this taxed Hudson's skills as a navigator to the limit.

Meanwhile, the crewmen had their own hardships. As they sailed farther north they encountered thick fog, followed by rough, stormy seas. Ice crusted the rigging and the sails froze. Whenever adjustments were necessary, the men had to climb aloft with numb hands and on slippery footing. Men were soaked to the skin by driving rain and the spray of the sea, and once that happened there wasn't much chance to dry clothes out and really feel warm again.

On June 13, Hudson sighted the east coast of Greenland. The world's largest island, most of it sheathed in ice, was still a mystery to Europeans. No one was sure if it was one island or several, nor how far north it stretched.

For eight days Hudson followed the coast northward, always keeping land in sight. He saw some previously unrecorded geographic features and added them to his chart. He wrote in his journal of the relentlessly harsh weather and the desolate land he could see from his ship.

> We saw some land on head of us, and some ice. It
> being a thick fog, we steered away northerly. In
> the morning our sails and shrouds froze. All the
> afternoon evening it rained, and the rain froze.
> This was a very high land, the most part cov-
> ered with snow. The nether part was uncovered.
> At the top it looked reddish, and underneath a
> blackish clay, with much ice lying about it.

A current carried the *Hopewell* eastward and out of sight of the coast. This frustrated Hudson because of the difficulty in maintaining his bearings. In spite of the weather, he managed to hold his ship to a northerly course. The crew endured a miserable week of rain squalls and heavy seas. Then they sighted land again. Hudson noted it in his log as a newly discovered land, which he called Hold-with-Hope. He didn't know it was a more northerly part of the Greenland coast.

Hudson was excited about this discovery, but he chose his words carefully as he made the entry in his log. He had gone quite a long way off the course the Muscovy Company directors had instructed him to take, and now he had to justify that to his employers. He expressed his satisfaction at finding that Robert Thorne's theory seemed to be correct. The weather seemed to be getting warmer as he neared the North Pole.

"This land is very temperate to our feeling. It is a high mainland, nothing at all covered with snow; and the north part of that main highland was very high mountains, but we could see no snow upon them."

Hudson apparently did not realize that the weather was warming simply because it was late June. He was surprised to find land here at all, because according to the charts he had studied in

Richard Hakluyt's house, it should have been open sea. In his log, Hudson gave this as justification for disobeying his orders and sailing so far to the west.

> This might be held against us, being our fault for keeping such a westerly course. The chief reason for this course was our desire to see that part of Groneland [Greenland], which for all we knew, was unknown to any Christian; we thought it could as well have been open sea as land, in which case our passage to the Pole would have been mostly completed. We also hoped to have a westerly wind, which if we were closer to the shore would have been an onshore [easterly] wind. Considering we found land our charts made no mention of, we considered our labor so much more worthwhile. For what we could see, it appeared to be a good land, and worth exploring.

By now the *Hopewell* was sailing beneath the midnight sun. Hudson found it fascinating to have sunlight twenty-four hours a day. Some of the men in the crew complained that they could not sleep and became irritable. However, John Hudson and the younger crew members claimed that with the constant sunlight, they found they needed less sleep.

One afternoon John Colman, the first mate, excitedly called Hudson to the rail. A grampus, a fierce sea mammal related to dolphins and toothed whales, was swimming in circles around the ship. Soon the animal was joined by two others. Sailors of that time were notoriously superstitious, and several of the crew members immediately took the appearance of the three creatures as an evil omen. They wanted to return to England immediately. Hudson refused. He watched the animals for hours and made notes about them. Possibly they stayed close to the ship because the cook had thrown some galley garbage overboard.

Hudson sailed northeast from Greenland, setting a course for the North Pole. He constantly found his path blocked by ice. On June 27, Hudson spotted one of the islands of the Spitzbergen Archipelago. These islands had already been discovered by the Dutch explorer William Barents in 1596, but he had thought they were part of Greenland. Hudson decided to give the group the English name of Newland. Then he sailed in amongst the islands, hoping the archipelago might be a gateway through to that temperate sea that supposedly surrounded the Pole.

For two days the *Hopewell* tacked her way north through the barren, jagged, snow-covered islands. Shore ice and rocks forced Hudson to keep a safe distance, though he would have liked to have made a landing. Then on the evening of June 29, the worst storm the *Hopewell* had yet encountered came shrieking down from the north.

Hudson was in a trap! If a ship were caught in a storm out on the open ocean, she could ride out the turbulence. But in the midst of a group of islands, there was a great danger of the ship being smashed to pieces.

Hudson bellowed the order for all hands on deck. He took the *Hopewell* into an island cove that offered partial protection. Then he shouted to Colman to take in all sail, and Colman relayed the order to Collin. Men clambered up into the rigging and along the yards, clinging for dear life as they hauled in the sheets. If a man fell into that icy, swirling sea, he'd be lost forever.

Young was at the helm, and Hudson told him to lash the whipstaff down. Then the captain ordered the sea anchor to be cast out. This was not the big iron anchor that secured a ship in harbour. It was a huge canvas bag that acted something like a modern-day parachute. It trailed in the water behind the ship, filling up with water, and so acted as a drag, preventing the ship from being blown very far or very fast. Only when all of that was done did Hudson allow the men to go below in relays for some warmth and rest. He remained on his quarterdeck the whole time, watching to be sure his vessel did not drift out into the full onslaught of the storm, or be thrown against the island's rocky shore.

The storm did not let up until the following morning, and then it was followed by fog and snow. Hudson spent the next two weeks picking his way through the islands, charting them, constantly fighting what he called "our troublesome neighbours, ice with fog." The men saw whales, seals, and evidence of polar bears. As they sailed in and out of inlets, they had to be careful not to become "embayed"; trapped by ice that prevented them from sailing out to open water.

As the July days passed, the weather improved, though the *Hopewell* had to constantly steer clear of ice. Then on July 14, Hudson took the ship into a large bay. What he and the men saw was absolutely astounding. The bay was teeming with whales! Hundreds of them! The whales lay in pods or frolicked in the bay. They seemed to have no fear of the ship. As Hudson noted in his journal:

> In this bay we saw many whales, and one of our company having a hook and line overboard to try for fish, a whale came under the keel of our ship and made her held. Yet by God's mercy we had no harm, but the loss of the hook and three parts of the line.

Now Hudson had information that would delight his employers. Whaling was an extremely profitable business. Almost every part of a whale was marketable. Whale meat was considered a delicacy. Whale blubber produced oil that had hundreds of uses. Whale bone was a versatile building material. Whale teeth were as valuable as ivory. Most valuable of all were two products that came from sperm whales: One was spermaceti, which was used in the manufacture of candles, soap, cosmetics, and machine oil. The other was ambergris, a waxy substance that came from the sperm whale's digestive system. Ambergris was used in the manufacture of perfume, and was every bit as valuable as spices from the Far East.

Hudson could practically see the smiles on the faces of the Muscovy Company directors. Even if he did not find a Northeast Passage, this voyage would prove to be very profitable indeed. No one else knew about Whale Bay, the name he had already chosen. The Muscovy Company could send its own whaling ships up here. There were many seals, too, and seal pelts were valuable.

Hudson took the ship to within one hundred feet of the shore and dropped anchor. The Muscovy Company would need practical information about this island if they were to establish a whaling station here. He sent Collin, Colman, and two others ashore in the ship's gig, a small rowboat. The other sailors watched enviously as the four men rowed to the island. They hadn't set foot on dry land in two-and-a-half months, and longed for a chance to get off the ship, even for just a couple of hours.

But no sooner did the shore party scramble up onto the rocks and haul the gig up after them than there was a dramatic turn in the weather. One minute it had been pleasant, almost balmy. Then a raging gale blew in, almost out of nowhere. A howling wind tore across the sea outside the bay and piled up mountains of green water. Watching the massive swells in awe, Hudson was thankful that the *Hopewell* was not still out there.

Within the bay the waters rolled from the effect of the seething ocean beyond the entrance, but the island's high cliffs shielded this pocket of calm from the fury of the tempest. Nonetheless, Hudson decided to call the shore party back as a precaution. Before he could do that, a fog descended upon the bay as swiftly as darkness falling after sundown. The fog was so dense that Hudson could not see the tops of the masts, nor the prow of the ship.

Hudson was worried about the men who had gone ashore. The island was a strange, new place, and who knew what dangers might be lurking in this fog. Sailors lined the rail and called out. A few times Hudson thought he heard calls in response. But fog can play tricks with sound, and Hudson was not sure if he heard the voices of his men on shore, or the voices of the men on the ship echoing off the cliffs. For hours he waited and fretted.

Then, as suddenly as it had rolled in, the fog lifted, and beyond the bay the storm died down. Soon after, Hudson looked on with relief as the shore party launched the gig and rowed back to the *Hopewell*. The sailors cheered them as they climbed aboard. Hudson was delighted by the report Colman made to him, and the specimens the men had collected.

Colman said that it had been comfortably warm on the island, and there were two streams of fresh, clear water. They had seen flocks of geese, and tracks made by bears, foxes, and other animals. The men had picked up many deer antlers, whalebones, and the skull of a "morse" (walrus) that still had the tusks. They also had a rock, which Hudson was certain was pure coal.

Hudson could hardly believe his good fortune. Walrus tusks, like whales' teeth, were as valuable as ivory. Everything the Muscovy Company would need to support a whaling station was right here! Fresh water, wild game, and if he was right about the coal, a source of fuel!

Having marked Whale Bay's position on his chart, Hudson weighed anchor and set sail that evening. July was half over, and he still had not reached the North Pole. He sailed north of the Spitzbergens to 80 degrees 23', the farthest north any European was known to have ventured up to that time. He could not find a break in the pack ice that blocked his way. Hudson wrote in his log, "Everywhere there is an abundance of ice compassing us about by the north and joining to the land." There was no way through to the Pole. Some of the men wanted to turn back for England.

But Hudson was not about to give up. He told the crew they were going to sail south, go around the Spitzbergens, and then up the east side of the islands and try again. There were grumblings from the crew, but Hudson ignored them.

For ten days the *Hopewell* followed an erratic course down the west side of the islands. Hudson had to constantly shift direction as the crew battled heavy winds, driving rain, and thick fog. On July 27, the crew of the *Hopewell* faced near disaster.

Throughout the voyage, whenever the ship was within sight of ice, Hudson wisely kept his distance. The *Hopewell* was a stout little ship, but a collision with the granite-like ice could have cracked her hull open like an eggshell. For several days, as they tacked back and forth, the crew saw no ice. Then the day came that none of them would ever forget.

The *Hopewell* was shrouded in fog, rain was falling, and the wind was light. The sea was calm, but the ship rose and fell on a heavy swell. Visibility was nil, so Hudson ordered reduced sails. As the ship was carried along on the swells, a low rumbling

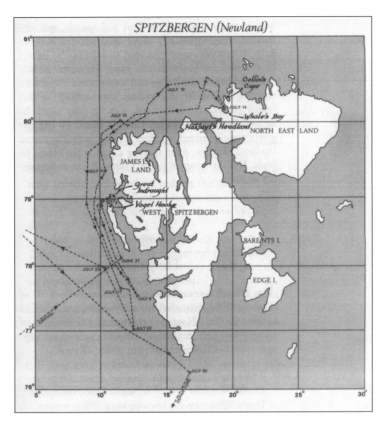

Map of the Spitzbergen Islands.

noise came out of the grey murk. It sounded like waves striking a shore. But Hudson knew they were not near enough to any land to hear the crash of surf.

The noise grew louder, and Hudson realized that the swells were carrying the *Hopewell* toward the source. Could there be yet another uncharted island out in the fog? Hudson shouted to the helmsman to alter course. He sent men aloft to put out more sail. But without a good breeze the sails were useless. All attempts to change the ship's direction with the whipstaff were to no avail.

The sound of crashing surf became thunderous. One sailor shouted for God's mercy. Another voice cursed Hudson for leading them to their doom.

Then, through a fleeting window in the fog, Hudson saw the ice pack! It looked as solid and menacing as a wall of rock. Huge rollers were smashing against it in explosions of white foam and spray. The growls and groans of the ice slabs grinding against each other were like a din from hell. The *Hopewell* was heading straight for that ice, carried along like a piece of driftwood.

Hudson sensed panic spreading through the crew. "Launch the gig!" he ordered.

Colman cried, "Captain, there isn't enough room in the gig for all of us, and what chance ..."

Hudson cut him off. "Don't question my orders, Mr. Colman," he barked angrily. "Launch the gig! We're not abandoning ship! I want a line fastened to the bow, with the other end to the gig. Put your six strongest rowers in the gig. Do it, man! Now!"

Colman thought the plan was hopeless, but with the ice looming ever closer, he obeyed the captain. When the gig was in the water with six strong oarsmen in it, Colman started to climb over the rail to take his place in the little boat's stern. Hudson pushed him aside.

"Get to the quarterdeck, Mr. Colman," Hudson ordered. "We'll tow her out of danger. You keep her steady."

Hudson climbed into the gig and told the rowers, "Now lads, if you want to see England again, put your backs to it."

Soon the gig was in front of the *Hopewell*, and the rope between them was stretched taut. The prow of the ship came around as the rowers warped her to starboard. But they seemed to be making no headway against the ceaseless movement of the swells.

Hudson told the men to row harder, and they did. But what was their strength against the power of the sea? The *Hopewell* was getting closer to the grinding jaws of ice, dragging the gig and its struggling rowers.

From his place on the quarterdeck Colman saw that the ship had been drawn into the outer fringes of the ice pack. White slabs bumped against the hull. They were like teeth that threatened to chew the timbers into splinters. Colman sent men to the rails to push the ice away with pikes and oars. The mate also said a silent prayer, because he was certain that the *Hopewell* and all her company would soon be at the bottom of the sea.

In the gig, Hudson urged the men on. But chunks of ice surrounded the boat and got in the way of the oars. The rowers lost their rhythm as each man struggled to get his oar in the water without striking ice. The thunder of the surf was almost deafening. Then the line that attached the gig to the ship went slack. "Captain!" one man cried in alarm. "They've cut us loose!"

Standing on the *Hopewell*'s quarterdeck, Colman looked up in thankful astonishment as the sails billowed. "God has answered my prayer!" he said to himself. A strong wind had suddenly blown in from the northwest. The sails that Hudson had ordered unfurled now bloomed full, and the *Hopewell* surged forward, away from the ice. The line to the gig had fallen slack because the ship was overtaking the boat. Soon the men who had tried so heroically to tow the ship clambered aboard and hauled in the gig. Later, when the ice and its horrific noise were far behind, Hudson made an entry in his log.

If not for the delivery by God of a northwest by west wind — a wind not commonly found on this voyage — it would have been the end of our voyage. May God give us thankful hearts for so great a deliverance.

Hudson had to admit defeat. It was not possible to sail past the North Pole to reach China. When he announced to the crew that they were returning to England, the men raised such a loud cry of joy that seabirds near the ship were frightened away. But Hudson's course did not take the *Hopewell* directly home. He made a four hundred-mile detour to the west, and discovered a previously uncharted island, which he called Hudson's Tutches. Today it is called Jan Mayen Island.

Hudson's journal offers no explanation as to why he went so far off course. It's not likely that bad weather was the cause. It could be that Hudson intended to spend a winter on the coast of Greenland, and then sail west to seek the Northwest Passage through the Furious Overfall. If that was his plan, one thing could have prevented him from following it. His men refused to go!

It will never be known if Hudson's crew threatened mutiny on his first important voyage, and demanded that he take them home. They had been to what was then considered the ends of the earth, and had fulfilled the obligations they had agreed to when they signed aboard. If Hudson did indeed try to push his men into a voyage of discovery to the west, he would have been demanding too much of them. On September 15, the *Hopewell* docked at Tilbury on the River Thames.

3

To Novaya Zemlya

As Hudson had predicted, the Muscovy Company was overjoyed to hear about the whales, walruses, and seals at Spitzbergen. The directors immediately began preparations for a whaling expedition the following year. Word got out, and the value of Muscovy Company stock tripled. If he accomplished nothing else, Hudson would go down in history as the father of the English whaling industry. Spies carried the news of Hudson's discovery to The Netherlands, France, Spain, and Portugal. Those countries would send whaling fleets of their own to the far north. The Dutch government sent a formal letter of protest to King James I, claiming that the islands were Dutch by right of prior discovery. James ignored the letter, and issued a royal decree claiming the islands for England (the islands are now under the jurisdiction of Norway).

The Muscovy Company and its shareholders profited enormously from Henry Hudson's voyage, but Hudson did not. There was nothing in the contract he had signed that said he was entitled to share in any wealth his discoveries generated, and the Muscovy men did not feel compelled to offer him anything. They made the king a gift of two thousand pounds worth of shares, but that was a matter of diplomacy. It was always a good idea to be in good favour with the king. Hudson, on the other hand, was a sea captain who had been paid to do a job.

Hudson probably wasn't concerned about being left out of the financial windfall his discovery had generated, though Katherine might have had a few things to say about it. Whatever faults Hudson had, avarice wasn't one of them. Getting rich was not as important to him as exploration.

After making his report to the Muscovy Company, Hudson went to Bristol to confer with Richard Hakluyt. Because he had been unable to penetrate the ice pack and sail to the North Pole, Hudson thought his voyage had been a failure. Hakluyt did not agree. He believed Hudson had made a considerable contribution to knowledge about the Arctic. He had disproven some old theories about the north, and he had filled in some of the empty spaces on the map of the world. To Hakluyt, that was more valuable than gold.

Hudson could easily have had a job with the Muscovy Company as captain of the Spitzbergen whaling fleet. But Hakluyt knew that employment of that nature would be too routine and tame for a man like Hudson, who had the urge to explore in his blood. He had some charts and documents that he thought might be of interest to his friend. They had to do with a mysterious place called Novaya Zemlya, a possible key to the Northeast Passage.

Novaya Zemlya consists of two large islands north of Russia. They are an extension of the Ural Mountains, which are considered the dividing line between Europe and Asia. These islands,

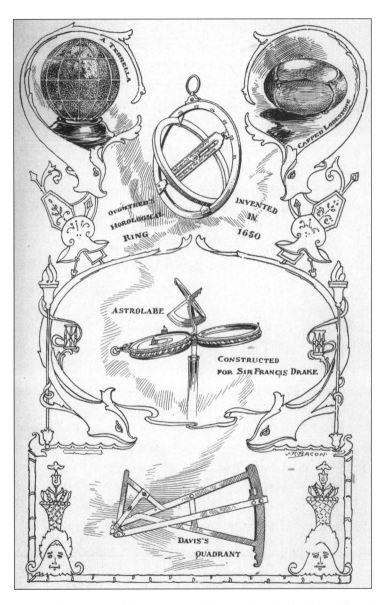

Devices that were used by mariners and geographers in the sixteenth and seventeenth centuries.

which would make a long peninsula were they not separated from the mainland, have the Barents Sea to the west and the Kara Sea to the east. The southern island (Yuzhny) is separated from the larger northern island (Severny) by a narrow channel called the Matochkin Strait. To the south of Yuzhny is the Kara Strait (also called the Burrough Strait). Then there is a small island called Vaigach, which is separated from the mainland by Pet Strait.

Sir Hugh Willoughby, an English explorer, had reported on the existence of Novaya Zemlya in 1553, and another Englishman, Stephen Borough, had landed there in 1556. William Barents had been there in 1596. Nonetheless, very little was known of this frozen land in an icy sea. Western Europeans knew almost nothing about the Kara Sea. The one fact they were certain of was that a six hundred mile long land mass north of Russia was a barrier in the path of a Northeast Passage to Cathay. Hakluyt had sent an emissary to St. Petersburg to see if he might learn more about the place. But people in Tsarist Russia were forbidden to give foreigners any information about their country. To break that law was to risk having your tongue cut out. If anyone in St. Petersburg had valuable information on Novaya Zemlya, they kept it to themselves.

Hakluyt and his Dutch colleague, Peter Plancius, had ignored the rivalry that now existed between their countries, and shared what sketchy information they had on Novaya Zemlya. Much of that came from ancient Norse legends. But Plancius knew that Barents (who had died in 1597) had seen the Kara Sea, though he did not know if Barents had actually sailed around Novaya Zemlya or had crossed it overland.

Most of Stephen Borough's log had been lost, but Hakluyt had a copy of a surviving fragment in which Borough claimed that a "placid sea" lay to the east of Novaya Zemlya. Hakluyt felt he had sound reason to believe in the existence of that ice-free sea. He knew that a mighty Russian river, the Ob, flowed into the sea east of Novaya Zemlya. Might the Ob be a potential route to China? Hakluyt knew something else. Someone had found a six foot long ivory horn on Vaigat Island. This was actually the tusk from a narwhal, an Arctic sea mammal that was practically unknown to Western Europeans. Hakluyt and most of his contemporaries who knew of this fantastic object believed it was a unicorn's horn. According to an account written at that time, the unicorn horn was proof that, "there must of necessity be a passage out of the said Oriental Ocean into our Septentrional (northern) seas." It was a well-known fact, the report said, "that unicorns are bred in the lands of Cathay, China and other Oriental Regions." In the early seventeenth century, even a learned man like Richard Hakluyt could be taken in by a myth.

Hakluyt shared all of this information with Hudson. The explorer was especially excited by the chart William Barents had made of the western shore of Novaya Zemlya. The eastern shore had not yet been mapped, but Barents' chart showed what appeared to be the entrance of a channel (the Matochkin Strait). No one knew if it connected to the Kara Sea. Hudson wanted to find out. He was willing to risk his life on another voyage of discovery. Would the Muscovy Company be willing to risk some money?

Aside from the fact that Hudson had meetings with Richard Hakluyt, nothing is known of his time in England after his first major voyage. No doubt he and John spent long hours at home, telling the family about their adventures in northern seas. Katherine and the others probably listened breathlessly to the story about the ice pack that almost took the *Hopewell* and all of her crew. They would have believed, as Hudson did, that the hand of God had spared them. Indeed, this might have given the family some comfort. The Hudsons would have been thankful in their belief that God was watching over Henry and John. No sailors needed divine protection more than those who sailed into the unknown. Henry Hudson was about to do just that again.

Hudson was confident when he met the Muscovy Company directors in their headquarters on Budge Row. He knew very well how valuable the Whale Bay discovery was to them. But he also knew that these were men for whom there could never be enough money. The possibility of trade with the Far East was still a golden beacon to them. Hudson did not tell them everything he had learned from Hakluyt. His nuggets of information were his best cards. He told them only that he possessed secret information about a Northeast Passage.

The businessmen conferred. Hudson had done well by them on his first voyage. If there was a chance he could still find a Northeast Passage, it was worth taking a chance with him again. They asked Hudson if he would be willing to make the voyage in the *Hopewell,* and for the same amount of money he had been paid for the first voyage. Hudson agreed, but this time he had some conditions of his own.

Hudson said he would need a larger crew. Arctic sailing added to the sailors' hardships and duties. He asked for five extra men. The directors frowned at the idea of having to pay another five sailors. They protested that a little ship like the *Hopewell* did not need so many men. They finally, grudgingly, agreed to increase the crew by three.

Then Hudson said he wanted the hull of the *Hopewell* reinforced with extra planking for protection from ice. Once again the directors howled with indignation. They asked Hudson if he was aware of the costs this would involve. Could he not simply sail around the ice? Hudson reminded the merchants that he had been up there, and knew better than they the hazards ice presented. Would it not be better, he asked, for them to spend whatever it cost to strengthen the ship, than to have the hull pierced by ice and lose the entire ship? Again, with much grumbling, the Muscovy men said they would strengthen the *Hopewell*'s hull.

Hudson wasn't finished. He told the directors that the *Hopewell*'s gig was inadequate. It was too frail for proper inshore exploration, he said. It was also too small for the entire crew should it ever be necessary to abandon ship. Hudson wanted the *Hopewell* equipped with a full sized ship's boat; a shallop, twenty-five to thirty feet long.

This was too much for the directors. They wailed that Captain Hudson seemed to have forgotten that they were men of business; that businesses operated on the basis of profit; that frivolous expenditures undermined profit and sent companies spiralling into bankruptcy. The *Hopewell*'s gig, they insisted, was a perfectly good craft. They refused to replace it with a larger, more expensive boat. Hudson bade them good day and left the office. The following morning a messenger arrived at Hudson's house with a letter from the Muscovy Company requesting the captain's presence at the office on Budge Row. The merchants had agreed to the ship's boat.

While the *Hopewell* was undergoing renovations, Hudson began selecting a crew. Besides his son John, the only crewmembers from the first voyage to sign on for this new expedition were John Cooke, whom Hudson promoted to bos'un, and James Skrutton. The new crew was made up of the ship's cook, John Branch, and seamen Arnold Ludlowe, John Adrey, Michael Perce, Richard Tomson, and Robert Raynor. Three other new men were possibly from prominent families. Thomas Hilles may have been related to a family that owned a fleet of merchant ships and provided financial insurance for walrus hunting expeditions. He might have been along to look into the prospects of harvesting walrus on Novaya Zemlya. John Barnes could have been from a Barnes family that was associated with the Muscovy Company. If so, he might have been sent to look after the company's interests. Humfrey Gilby might have been a relative of the late explorer Sir Humphrey Gilbert. After his first voyage, Hudson was something of a celebrity, and it would not be unusual for well-to-do families to send young men on a voyage with him to gain knowledge and experience.

The last two members of the crew were men with whom Hudson's destiny would be dramatically bound. One was Philip Staffe. All that is known of him is that he was a ship's carpenter; probably a big man with considerable physical strength. On a wooden sailing ship there was always something in need of repair. Staffe would have been seen as a step above the common seaman.

Then there was Hudson's new mate, Robert Juet. Probably in his fifties when he joined the crew of the *Hopewell*, Juet evidently came from the north of England — possibly even Scotland. Juet lived in Limehouse, a working class district in the east end of London that was popular with seamen. But unlike most of the mariners who lived in that rough part of town, Juet was literate and possibly even well-educated. The fragments of his journal that have survived show that he knew mathematics and was familiar with books on navigation.

There is no doubt that Robert Juet was an experienced and skilled mariner. He had most likely spent most of his life at sea. He knew how to use all of the latest nautical instruments, was knowledgeable in up-to-date theories on navigation, and was, in fact, a first class navigator, perhaps even better than Hudson. Why then was Robert Juet, who was Hudson's senior in age by at least ten years, not a captain? The answer to that question quite likely lay in Juet's personality.

Observations made about Juet by other people, and the attitude that underlies statements in his own writings, reveal Juet as a most unpleasant individual; a man who, in spite of his exceptional skills, could not be trusted with command of a ship. He seems to have been, by his very nature, cynical, quarrelsome, envious, and insubordinate. Juet was a born troublemaker. There is no record of how Henry Hudson met Robert Juet or why he signed him on as second in command of the *Hopewell*. No doubt Juet's credentials looked impressive. His advanced knowledge of navigation might have caused Hudson to see him as a good man to have on board. There is also the possibility that the Muscovy Company hired Juet as mate and then thrust him upon Hudson. It was the beginning of a relationship that was not only odd, but also very dangerous. Before the *Hopewell* even sailed, Hudson wrote a letter to Hakluyt in which he said Robert Juet "is filled with mean tempers." Bad feelings between the captain and his first officer did not bode well for a successful voyage.

The Muscovy Company had given Hudson a free hand in equipping and provisioning the *Hopewell*. The merchants groaned as the bills arrived in the office on Budge Row. Hudson had purchased large quantities of salted and pickled meat, which cost considerably more than grain and dried peas. He had observed during his first Arctic voyage that a diet without much meat had made his men weak. He concluded that men working in cold weather required more meat to help keep their strength up.

Hudson also convinced the Muscovy Company to provide arms for the *Hopewell*. He wanted a musket for every member of the crew, and a supply of powder and shot. He also purchased a small cannon, which was kept under lock and key in his quarters. Considering that firearms were very expensive, Hudson must have presented some pretty strong arguments for the merchants to purchase them. Perhaps he was concerned that there might be trouble if they ran into any Russians who objected to having Englishmen trespassing on their territory. Or Hudson might have thought that if they reached the Pacific Ocean, they might be vulnerable to attack by Oriental pirates.

On April 22, 1608, the *Hopewell* was ready to sail. That morning, as was the custom of the time, an Anglican clergyman went aboard to say a prayer for the captain and crew, and to ask God's blessing for the voyage. Juet did not attend the religious service. He was in his cabin entertaining friends. The more devout members of the crew would have found it distressing that the ship's mate would miss a formal ceremony that sought God's protection for ship and crew.

Hudson finally had to send Juet's guests ashore so the *Hopewell* could sail on the afternoon tide. Juet was not happy about that. Hudson wrote in his journal, "The nose of Master Juet was put much out of joint. When I desired to retire to my sleeping-cabin, J. was still in foul humours, and had to be summoned to take the watch."

During the first month of the voyage north nothing disturbed workaday life aboard the ship. Then, as the *Hopewell* approached the Lofoten Islands off the west coast of Norway, the vessel sailed into thick fog and the temperature plummeted. Hudson recorded that it was "searching cold," which probably meant that the icy cold seemed to search through a man's clothing to chill him to the bone. It was no doubt the cold that caused several of the crewmen to fall ill. Philip Staffe was so sick, he was confined to his hammock for several days.

By June 24, clear and relatively warm weather had replaced the fog and the cold. Hudson sighted Norwegian fishing boats. Staffe had recovered enough to go back to work, so Hudson told him to make a mast for the shallop. If the ship's boat were fitted with a sail, it would be faster, and the oarsmen would be spared a great deal of labour.

Like all wind-driven ships, the *Hopewell* carried spare canvas sails. Every sail was cut and rigged to suit a specific purpose. None of the *Hopewell's* extra sails was a proper fit for the shallop. Hudson ordered Juet to supervise the cutting and sewing of a new sail.

Juet objected. Sailmaking, he argued, was not one of a mate's duties. Hudson reminded Juet that the captain, not the mate, was the ship's master. He said that he had replaced his mate on a previous voyage, and would do so again if necessary.

A pair of unhappy sailors cut and stitched the shallop's sail under Juet's critical eye. When it was finished, Hudson praised it as a job well done. But Juet seethed with anger. The captain had threatened to demote him! Robert Juet had served under many captains, and given his dreadful nature he might not have liked any of them. Now he was finding reasons to dislike Henry Hudson.

On June 8, as the ship rounded North Cape, Norway, Hudson noticed that the colour of the sea was a distinctive black. Drawing on his experiences of the previous year, Hudson concluded that he was approaching ice, though no ice was visible. The next day his theory was confirmed when the lookout shouted that ice lay ahead. Hudson was the first mariner known to make the scientific observation that the proximity of ice affects the colour of the sea. He took his ship in among the floes, hoping to cautiously pick his way through them. No doubt he was glad he'd had the *Hopewell's* hull reinforced, as he recorded experiencing "a few rubs of our ship against the ice." After several tense hours the ship emerged safely from the other side of the ice pack. On June 15, two of Hudson's men made a not-so-scientific observation. They reported seeing a mermaid. Hudson wrote of the incident:

> This morning one of our crew while looking overboard saw a mermaid [and called] the rest of the crew to come see her. One more [crew-man] came up; by that time she was close to the ship's side and looking earnestly at the men; a little after a sea came up and overturned her. As they saw her, from the naval upward, her back and breasts were like a woman's, her body as big as ours, her skin very white, and she had long, black hair hanging down behind. In her going down they saw her tail, which was like the tail of a porpoise, and speckled like a mack-erel. Thomas Hiles [*sic*] and Robert Rayner [*sic*] were the men who saw her.

It is not surprising that Hudson would so unquestioningly accept a report that two of his men had seen a mermaid. At that time, people believed that for every creature that lived on the land there was a corresponding creature in the sea. Hence, sea-horse, sea lion, and, of course, sea folk — or, in their terminol-ogy, mer-people — were believed real. For thousands of years mariners had been mistaking sea animals like seals, dolphins, dugongs, and manatees for mermaids and mermen. Hudson would not have questioned the existence of mermaids anymore than Hakluyt questioned the existence of unicorns.

Hudson continued his northerly course until June 18, when he once again faced the great barrier of ice that had thwarted him the previous summer. Across the open water came that chilling din of ice floes smashing and grinding against each other, sounding as if the great white mass was a monster hungry for a ship to devour. Hudson could sense uneasiness in the crew.

Hudson sailed along the edge of the ice, looking for an opening. He found none, and was forced to turn southeast. Two days later he recorded that they had seen an astonishing number of seals and had heard bears roaring on the ice. He was surprised to see great flocks of seabirds so far north. Their numbers indicated that this must be a rich fishing ground. The weather was alternately clear and foggy, but very cold. The sails froze.

On June 26, the lookout sighted land. Hudson knew from his charts that they were approaching Novaya Zemlya. Because of the impassable ice, sailing north and going around the tip of the island was out of the question. Hudson decided to search for the channel that supposedly cut through the land mass.

Hudson sailed south, keeping a safe two miles offshore. On June 27, he dropped anchor in a shallow cove. He already suspected that there was no navigable Northeast Passage to be found here. Should Hudson's fears be confirmed, he needed something of value to take back to the Muscovy Company, as he had done a year earlier with his discovery of Whale Bay. After all the expense Hudson had put the merchants to for this voyage, if he went home empty-handed it might well be his ruin. He wrote in his log:

> June 27, 1608. We being two miles from the shore, I sent my mate Robert Juet and John Cooke my boatswain on shore, with four others, to see what the land would yield that might

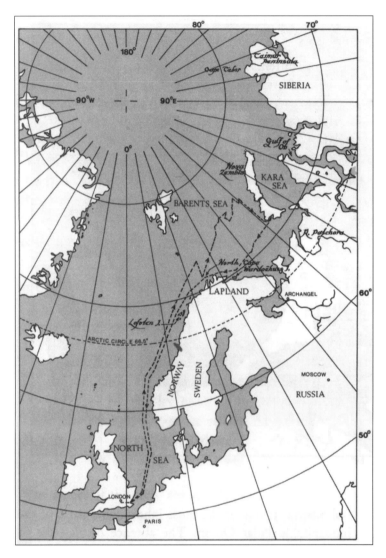

Map of Nova Zemlaya (called Zembla in Dutch), with detail of Hudson's 1607 route.

be profitable and to fill two or three casks with water. They found and brought aboard some whales' fins, two deer's horns, and the dung of deer and they told me they saw grass on the shore of the last years, and young grass come up amongst it.

It was very hot on the shore, and the snow melted apace, they saw the footings of many great bears, of deer and foxes. We saw two or three companies of morses near us swimming.

There was a cross standing on the shore, much driftwood, and signs of fires that had been made there.

The remains of campfires could have been left by Inuit hunters, but the cross was evidence that Russians visited this remote place. Hudson couldn't be sure what sort of welcome he and his men would get from either group if they were found. Novaya Zemlya was holding less appeal for him all the time.

Other crewmen requested permission to go ashore. The following day Hudson sent Juet, Staffe, Arnold Ludlowe, and a few others to explore a different part of the island. These men returned with a whale's fin, some water fowl they had killed, and several eggs, some of which were good to eat. They had also gathered some small, sweet-scented flowers of a type not known in England. Hudson pressed some of the flowers between the pages of a book, because he knew Hakluyt would want to study them. But so far, Hudson hadn't found anything that would impress his employers.

The waters in this area were full of walrus, and Hudson thought that if he could take a large harvest of tusks back to London, some of the costs of the expedition would be covered.

However, the walrus were all in the water, and not on the land where they could be hunted.

Hudson decided to follow the animals to where they went ashore. To do this he had the sails taken in, and put men in the shallop to tow the *Hopewell*. This was safer than trusting the wind so close to shore in unfamiliar waters.

On June 30, Hudson saw about fifty walrus basking in the sun on a small island that was not much more than a rock jutting out of the ocean. He dropped anchor. To the men's great joy, the captain ordered everybody ashore to kill walrus! Only Hudson and his son remained on board the ship.

Hudson watched from the rail as the shallop, propelled by strong oarsmen, shot across the water toward the little island. He was thankful that he had stood his ground with the Muscovy merchants on the matter of the ship's boat. It was big enough to accommodate all of the crew, and much more durable in these rough, rock-strewn waters than that pitiful little gig had been.

Reproduction of The Chase of the Walrus, *by G. Hartwig.*

The crewmen reached the island, piled out of the boat, and ran toward the walrus, their clubs and pikes ready for the slaughter. As Hudson looked on, his vision of a treasure in walrus tusks quickly evaporated. His men were not skilled hunters. If they had been, they would have approached the animals in such away as to not alarm them too soon, and they would have cut off the walrus' retreat to the sea. Hudson was also astounded by the speed with which the awkward-looking creatures could move when they were threatened.

As soon as the walrus heard the whooping sailors, the entire herd headed straight for the water, the huge bodies undulating as they seemed to roll down the rock face of the island. They dove in with a spray of white water and vanished. Then, at a safe distance from the shore, heads popped up on the surface and barked in protest at the men who had disturbed their rest. The sailors managed to catch only one walrus that had been too far from the water. Three or four men ran pikes through its body while another struck it on the head with a club. Then they cut off the head to take back to the captain. Before leaving the island the sailors killed a large sea bird and gathered a quantity of eggs for the cook's larder. Back on the ship, John Hudson heard his father curse under his breath over the loss of the ivory.

On July 1, Hudson saw what appeared to be the mouth of a large river at the head of a bay. He tossed a marker over the side, and the speed with which it was carried told Hudson that the current here was strong. He thought that the river mouth might actually be the entrance to the channel he sought. If so, the expedition might yet be a success! Hudson dropped anchor in the bay and began to make preparations for some local exploration.

An anchor is simply an iron weight designed to hold a ship in one place in shallow water. But in heavy seas or a strong current, the force of the water can carry a ship along anyway, dragging the anchor across the bottom. For those situations, anchors have hook-like flues that catch on rocks and hold the ship secure. But if the bottom is smooth, a ship can drift.

That's what happened to the *Hopewell*. Hudson had anchored in the current that came from the rivermouth, but he underestimated its strength. Dragging her anchor, the *Hopewell* was carried along until she ran aground on a shoal.

The ship lurched to a stop that shivered her timbers from fore to aft. On deck, men grabbed at anything that would break a fall. In the galley the cook stumbled and dropped a bowl full of seabird eggs. Off-duty sailors, trying to get some sleep, were thrown from their bunks. Everyone below decks and above heard the awful screech of oak on rock as the *Hopewell's* bottom slid onto the shoal. Fortunately, no men were in the rigging so no one was thrown into the frigid water. As soon as the ship stopped and the sailors could get their footing, men raced below to inspect the damage. Hudson immediately ordered the shallop to be readied, just in case.

A shoal is one of a sailor's worst nightmares — a sandbar or rock hidden by just a few feet of water. At that time, unless a shoal was marked on a chart, a captain didn't know it was there until his ship hit it. A ship that struck a shoal could have the hull ripped wide open and sink in minutes. Or the vessel could be "hung up"; helplessly stranded and left to the merciless battering of the waves.

Hudson was relieved to hear from Juet and Cooke that the *Hopewell* had taken no serious damage. But then, in a burst of temper, Juet shouted that *he* would not have dropped anchor in such a place! He said so right to Hudson's face, with Cooke and other crewmen looking on.

Bos'un Cooke was shocked. If a ship's officer had a dispute with the captain, he raised the matter privately behind close doors, not in front of the men. Juet had not only breached shipboard protocol, he had also questioned the captain's competence. Cooke fully expected to see Juet demoted on the spot.

But Hudson did not demote Juet. He looked at the mate coldly for a few seconds. Then he said in an even voice, "Mr. Juet, take ten men in the ship's boat and tow us free."

Juet fumed. But if he had anymore angry words to say, he kept them to himself. Juet followed his orders and went into the shallop with a company of oarsmen. With the help of a good wind the men pulled the *Hopewell* free. Later, in the captain's cabin, Hudson commended Juet for pulling the vessel off the shoal. He said he was willing to forget the mate's earlier insubordination. Juet replied that he, too, regretted the incident and would gladly forget it. But Juet was not a man who let bygones be bygones.

The next day Hudson sent Juet and a company of men in the shallop to explore the river mouth. When they returned Juet reported that the gap in the coast was wide. Soundings he had made with a lead-weighted line showed that the channel was deep enough to allow the *Hopewell* to pass through. He also said that the water tasted salty.

This was good news to Hudson. The water at a river mouth, where fresh water mixed with salt water, would taste brackish; not fresh, but not as salty as water from the open sea. That meant the opening was not the mouth of a river. Because of the strong current, Hudson was sure this was the channel he'd been searching for.

On July 5, Hudson sailed the *Hopewell* into the entrance, but a combination of strong current and a contrary wind prevented the ship from making any headway. He ordered Juet to take five men in the shallop and explore as far along the channel as they could. The men were provided with guns in case they encountered bears or unfriendly local people, and a two day supply of food. Juet didn't complain about being sent into that forbidding interior, and possibly having to spend a night or two sleeping on the cold ground instead of in the comfort of his cabin. But the sullen expression on his face told Hudson that the mate wasn't happy about it.

After the shallop had disappeared from sight, Hudson could do nothing but wait. As the hours passed, the men went about their duties quietly. But Hudson knew that they would be whispering about their shipmates out in that strange, lonely place, and wondering if they would see them alive again.

By the following morning there was no sign of the shallop. Hudson decided to try once more to sail the *Hopewell* into the channel. The wind had shifted slightly to the west, so he thought they might make better progress than they had the day before. For a short distance they did. Then the wind shifted again, and the *Hopewell* was forced back. The overall mood of the crew turned ugly.

Early in the afternoon the lookout spotted the shallop coming down the channel. Juet and the others were soon aboard, safe and sound. But the report the mate delivered was not what Hudson wanted to hear.

They had gone about twenty-four miles along the channel, and Juet took soundings all the way. The depth had become increasingly shallow, until they reached a point where the water was only a few feet deep. There was no passage there for a ship, Juet said. Before turning back, he had taken the men ashore and gathered some wild goose quills and samples of vegetation. Juet said the men had seen many deer.

The disappointment Hudson felt was crushing. Hakluyt would be thrilled with the information about the flora and wildlife on Novaya Zemlya, but Hudson had nothing for the Muscovy Company. The charts he had drawn of the Novaya Zemlya west coast were the most accurate that had been made up to that time. But the charts would mean nothing to the merchants if they didn't show a Northeast Passage to China — the passage whose secret location Hudson was supposed to have known. To the Muscovy men, maps that did not lead to financial profit were just wall decorations.

It is not certain if Hudson actually found the Matochkin Strait, but quite likely he did. Juet probably explored one-third of its sixty-mile length. The strait is frozen over most of the year, and is very narrow and shallow at the point where Juet allegedly turned back. Beyond that shallow part, the channel deepens again.

Hudson had thought that if the channel went all the way to the Kara Sea — which, in fact, it does — the deep bay at its western end would make a good harbour. He never knew how close he was to being right. If Juet had explored a little farther and found deep water again, it might have been possible for the strait to have become a link in a Northeast Passage route. For all his personal shortcomings, Juet could not be blamed for turning back. From his position, the channel had become too shallow to warrant further consideration. Most men would have done what Juet considered the sensible thing, and turned back.

Henry Hudson was different. He hated the idea of defeat, and the fact that the northern ice had beaten him once again made him all the more determined. For several days he cruised back and forth along the coast, looking for anything that might be a channel. The temperature dropped and the sails froze.

Strong winds whipped up the sea. When the crewmen weren't being soaked with rain they were being pelted with hail.

One day Hudson saw what appeared to be the entrance to a channel, but the waters were so choked with ice that the ship could not get near it (this was actually a gap between Novaya Zemlya and a smaller island). Hudson wrote in his log, "It is so full of ice, you would hardly believe it. All day it was foggy and cold."

The Muscovy merchants would read Hudson's journal thoroughly, so he had to use language that would impress upon them the extreme conditions that prevented him from finding the Northeast Passage. He also alluded to the prevailing belief that all sea ice was formed in fresh water, when he explained that the ice in the northern seas came from the many rivers in Novaya Zemlya, Russia, and Greenland. Then he wrote, "By means of which ice I suppose there will be no navigable passage this way."

That sentence was an admission of failure, no matter how Hudson tried to colour it. Sitting alone in his cabin, he studied his charts, pondering how he might rescue the expedition, as well as his professional reputation. An idea came to him. Then he admitted to himself that the idea had been there all along, waiting for the search for a Northeast Passage to prove to be an empty quest. It was a risky idea that Hudson knew he had better keep to himself for the time being. There was nothing dishonest about that, he reasoned. He was master of the *Hopewell*, and a captain was not obliged to share all of his thoughts with the crew. Hudson did not even intend to consult with his officers, especially not with Juet.

The following day the men saw the nesting ground of hundreds of large sea birds, which Hudson called "wellocks" (these could have been any of the ducks, geese, swans, or gulls that nest here). He sent the bo'sun ashore with a hunting party of five men armed with muskets to shoot as many birds as they could. They returned with over a hundred fat wellocks. John Branch, the cook, quickly put men to work plucking, gutting and cleaning the birds, and salting them down. But Hudson instructed him to roast a few of the biggest and most succulent right away, and serve the men a delicious feast. The crewmen were greatly cheered to have a break from the monotonous fare of salted meat, porridge, and biscuits. But Robert Juet, while he enjoyed his supper, suspected that Hudson was up to something.

Hudson's journal is not clear about what happened next. On or about July 12, he announced to the crew that they were leaving Novaya Zemlya and sailing for England. The men were overjoyed that the cold, miserable Arctic conditions would soon be behind them. As the *Hopewell* sailed west, away from the ice, Hudson noted in his log that the sailors welcomed the sight of a green sea, after so many weeks on the forbidding, black waters that skirted the ice barrier. They were delighted to see porpoises leaping through the swells, because that was a sure sign of more temperate seas.

By July 30, the *Hopewell* was off Norway's Lofoten Islands. Hudson had a clear course south to England. But he didn't take it. Instead, he turned west, evidently thinking that no one in the crew would be the wiser. Hudson had decided to take ship and crew to North America and search for the Northwest Passage! He intended to enter the Furious Overfall, and sail three hundred miles along its course to see if it was, in fact, a Northwest Passage. He knew the crew would not be happy with his decision, but he would deal with that problem when the time came.

Apparently, Hudson plotted a course for Labrador. Even the lowliest sailor knew how to tell direction from the position of the sun, so Hudson must have had an explanation for why they were sailing toward the setting sun, when it should have been to the starboard (right) of the ship. The men were not fooled for long. Juet could take a reading just as well as Hudson, and it was probably he who realized, about August 6, that they were not headed for home.

Upon learning that they were heading for America, the crewmen would have been angry, not only because they were not on the way home, but also because Hudson had deceived them. Evidently the men threatened to mutiny, in all likelihood led by Juet. They would at least have required Juet's approval, because they would need him to navigate if Hudson proved uncooperative.

Hudson capitulated, but the crew wanted something more. They were very aware of the penalty they might pay for mutiny if Hudson decided to press charges when the ship reached London. Mutiny was as serious an offence as piracy, and the punishment was grim. The guilty were hanged, and then their bodies were gibbeted (hung in chains) by the London docks as a warning to other sailors. This concern of the would-be mutineers was the probable cause of a curious entry in Hudson's log.

> August 7. I used all diligence to arrive at London, and therefore I now gave my crew a certificate under my hand, of my free and willing return, without force or persuasion by any one or more of them. For when we were at Nova Zembla on the 6th of July, void of hope of a Northeast Passage … I therefore resolved to use all means I could to sail to the northwest.

In this entry, Hudson admitted that he had made a try for the Northwest Passage. The fact that he made a point of saying that his crew did not force him to give up the attempt, indicates that they did, in fact, force him. Having persuaded Hudson to change course by threatening to mutiny if he didn't, the crew then demanded a written guarantee that Hudson would not have them arrested when they got home. The *Hopewell* arrived at Gravesend on August 26.

If there had been a threat of mutiny, and even in spite of the written guarantee, Hudson still could have had the men charged. He would simply have had to say that he had signed the guarantee under duress. The guilty parties would have been arrested, thrown into jail, tried before a judge, and then hanged. But Hudson did not press any charges. This, along with the fact that he gave in to the threat of a mutiny, would have marked Hudson as a weak captain in the eyes of his men, as well as others, once the story got around. There was no doubt that he was an accomplished navigator. There was no questioning his courage; cowards did not willingly sail into unknown seas. But a strong captain stood up to anyone who dared to challenge his authority aboard ship, with a sword if necessary. Or he used the power of the law to ensure that troublemakers did not get away with their crimes. Hudson did neither.

The reception Hudson had from the Muscovy Company was every bit as bad as he had feared it would be. The merchants were disappointed that Hudson had not found the Northeast Passage, whose secret he had claimed to know. They had gone to great expense for the voyage, and what had Hudson to show for it? News of walrus at Novaya Zemlya? That was interesting, but the whales at Spitzbergen were much closer. As for Hudson's meticulously drawn charts, what use were they if the Muscovy Company couldn't send trading vessels up there? The merchants thanked Hudson for his efforts, and then bade him good day.

Hudson felt that he was a failure. Samuel Purchas met him several times and said that Hudson was, "sunk into the lowest depths of the Humor of Melancholy, from which no man could rouse him. It mattered not that his Perseverance and Industry had made England the richer by his maps of the North. I told him he had created Fame that would endure for all time, but he would not listen to me."

Hakluyt, too, pointed out to Hudson the importance of the geographic and scientific knowledge he had brought back. The scholar was fascinated with the samples from the north that Hudson had brought him, and wrote page after page of his observations concerning them in a huge book. Knowledge, Hakluyt told Hudson, was worth more than all the gold and silver in a merchant's vault. Hudson could not have agreed more. But it was the gold and silver in merchants' vaults that paid for voyages of discovery.

Hudson tried to convince the Muscovy Company that if given a ship and a crew, he could find the Northwest Passage. The merchants were not interested. Moreover, there was gossip on the docks and in the taverns that Hudson had allowed himself to be intimidated by his crew. How much truth there was to the rumour, they could not be sure. But Hudson's reputation as a captain and navigator was certainly not as esteemed as it had been before he set off on his second voyage. However, if Hudson's name had lost some of its renown in England, such was not the case across the water in continental Europe. Men in two rival nations would soon be very anxious indeed to talk to Henry Hudson.

4

Dutch Intrigues

In the early seventeenth century, Europe was in a great state of change. For most of the sixteenth century, Spain and Portugal had been the dominant powers. They carved out empires in the New World, and their ships controlled the only known, and very long, sea routes to the Far East. But the Protestant Reformation — a revolt against the power of the Roman Catholic Church — and wars of succession among the ruling dynastic families of Europe, brought about social and political upheaval. King Philip II of Spain, claiming to be the rightful heir to the Portuguese throne, invaded Portugal and made himself king there in 1580. As a result, Portuguese ships were in the Spanish Armada that met with disaster in the English Channel. Portugal had lost its independence to Spain, and both countries were weakened by the incredible military loss to England.

Meanwhile, religious differences threw Europe into turmoil as people either converted to Protestantism or remained loyal to the Catholic Church and the pope. Which religion a person accepted was not a matter of personal choice. Governments made the decisions. Subjects or citizens who did not follow the religion accepted by the state were often brutally persecuted. Both sides were guilty of vicious, bloody atrocities. Spain, Portugal, and France remained mostly Catholic. England, Scotland, and many of the German principalities became mainly Protestant. So did the Dutch-speaking people of the Netherlands, a region of northwestern Europe that was part of Spain's continental empire. Declaring all Protestants to be heretics, the Spanish were ruthless in their attempts to stamp out Protestantism in the Netherlands. The Dutch rebelled. After many years of fighting, they were able to throw off the Spanish yoke.

Even before the Netherlands forced Spain to formally acknowledge its independence, Dutch traders were laying the foundations of a commercial empire. Dutch merchant ships plied the seas, carrying the products of all nations to distant ports of call. Since the Portuguese were no longer able to protect their sea lanes around Africa and their trading centres in the Far East, the Dutch moved in, winning from local rulers the same trading rights and protection from pirates that the Portuguese had enjoyed. Some Dutch sea captains became pirates themselves, and joined the English seadogs in preying on Spanish ships carrying the treasures of the New World from the Caribbean to Spain. The loot the Dutch pirates took home increased the Netherlands' ability to wage its insurrection against the Spanish.

The largest mercantile enterprise in the Netherlands was the Dutch East India Company. Unlike the Muscovy Company, which was an independent business in competition with rival

The symbol of the Dutch East India Company.

English merchant houses, the Dutch East India Company was made up of a group of trading firms that pooled their money and other resources into one corporation. The official name was *De Vereenigde Oost-Indische Compagnie* (Dutch East India Company). It was known by its Dutch initials, VOC.

The VOC had a charter from the Dutch Republic's ruling council, the *Staats-General*, that almost gave it the powers of a sovereign state. It held a virtual monopoly on Dutch international trade and could negotiate treaties with foreign powers. That was something an English company could not do without first obtaining the consent of the king. The VOC had legal authority to mount overseas expeditions on its own initiative, establish colonies, and even maintain an army and wage war. It had its own fleet of ships armed with five hundred cannons, and employed about five thousand sailors. By the time of Hudson's second voyage to the Arctic, the VOC was one of the most powerful merchant companies in Western Europe, with financial resources the Muscovy Company could only dream of. Even though the VOC had a profitable trade route around Africa to the Far East, its directors shared the English belief that a shorter one might lie through a Northeast Passage. There was also a chance that the VOC could lose its southern route to the Orient. Negotiations for a peace settlement with Spain had been ongoing for years. One of Spain's conditions for recognizing Dutch independence was that the Dutch give up their around-Africa trading network. If the Dutch government caved in to that demand, the VOC would have a serious problem. Therefore, their agent in London had been keeping an eye on the Muscovy Company and the work of Henry Hudson.

The Muscovy Company had, in effect, fired Hudson, and he was despondent. He had a family to support and a house to keep up, and he was not a wealthy man. No doubt he could get a job as captain on a merchant ship. He might even take command of a slave ship. The trade in "black ivory," slaves captured along the west coast of Africa and sold in the New World, was growing steadily. There was a constant demand for captains and crews. The pay was good, if you could stand the tropical heat and survive the diseases of equatorial Africa. Neither of these prospects appealed to Hudson.

Sometime in the autumn of 1608, a Dutch diplomat named Emanuel Van Meteran went to Hudson's house. Van Meteran was an influential man in finances and politics. He had been the Dutch Consul in London for many years, and he was also an agent for the VOC. He had a network of spies who kept him up-to-date on just about everything that happened in London and other major English ports.

Van Meteran knew that Hudson was a captain in need of a ship and an expedition. Sitting in the explorer's study, he asked if Hudson was aware that the Dutch government had a standing offer of a reward of twenty-five thousand guilders (Dutch silver coins) for any man who could find a short route to China, by the east or the west. Hudson replied that he had heard of the prize. What navigator hadn't? Twenty-five thousand guilders was an incredible sum of money. But Hudson told his visitor that he did not believe a practical Northeast Passage existed. If there was such a passage at all, he explained, it was icebound and of no use as a shipping lane. The secret of the short route to the Orient, Hudson said, lay to the northwest.

Van Meteran left the house. A few days later he sent Hudson an invitation to join him for a meal at the Dutch Consulate. Hudson accepted, and over a fine supper Van Meteran said that he had associates in Amsterdam who were very interested in the travels of Henry Hudson. They wanted to meet him personally. He asked Hudson if he would like to go to Amsterdam. When Hudson was slow in responding, Van Meteran quickly added that all travel expenses would be paid. Hudson immediately accepted. He requested only that the trip be delayed until after the christening of his first grandchild, his son Oliver's daughter, Alice.

The ceremony was held at the Church of St. Mary Aldermary, on Bow Lane in London. Henry and Katherine were grandparents! Did Hudson wonder if perhaps he was getting too old to go venturing off into the unknown? Probably not. At that time the average life expectancy in England was forty-three years. Hudson did not know of that statistic. But he was certainly aware of the fact that life was short, and if a man wanted to make his mark, as Hudson did, he had to press on until infirmity or death stopped him.

A few days later, Hudson was aboard a ferry boat to Amsterdam. A letter that he wrote to Katherine provides an insight into what common passenger service was like in those days. "The odors below deck were so offensive to my nostrils," Hudson said, "that I begged the captain for the privilege of standing on his quarterdeck so I would not become ill." Apparently passengers who were not famous Arctic explorers had to remain below, out of the crew's way, and suffer.

Hudson knew that the VOC wanted to hire him for a voyage of discovery. He hoped they would want him to sail west. As far as he was concerned, there was no Northeast Passage.

Hudson had no reservations about working for foreign employers. That sort of thing happened all the time. Christopher Columbus had been a Genoese working for the Spanish. John and Sebastian Cabot had been Venetians working for the English, and Sebastian had gone into the employ of the Spanish. John Davis, the explorer who might have been Hudson's mentor, had sailed to the East Indies with the Dutch, only to be killed by Japanese pirates. There was nothing to prohibit an Englishman from selling his services to foreigners, as long as he did not work for a country with which England was at war. That would be viewed as treason, for which the penalty was death.

As a well-travelled mariner, Hudson had probably visited Amsterdam before, and was familiar with its harbour. Situated on the Zuider Zee, a shallow inlet sixty-two miles long and thirty-one miles wide, Amsterdam was one of the busiest ports in the world. Dozens of ships, many of them flying the orange white and blue banner of the VOC, lined the docks. They discharged cargoes of spices from the Far East, wine from Italy, wool from England, and timber from Scandinavia. More ships rode at anchor out in the harbour, waiting their turn to be unloaded. Small Dutch fishing boats returning from the North Sea wove their way through the flotilla of larger vessels toward the jetty where wholesalers would compete for the best of the catch.

The salt-tinged breeze carried a potent stew of smells; tar, spices, fish, wet canvas, wood smoke, and garbage. To Hudson's ears came a cacophony of noises that was to him the symphony of a bustling port: the slap of water against wooden hulls, the screeching of gulls, the shouts of Dutch dock workers and of sailors speaking a dozen different languages. To a landsman observing Amsterdam harbour for the first time, the whole scene would appear to be utter chaos. But Hudson knew that all around him, everything was working with typical Dutch efficiency.

When Hudson finally disembarked from the smelly little ferry boat, he found no one from the VOC waiting to meet him on the dock. He had not expected to be greeted. In an age when communications were poor and travel schedules unheard of, no one could know for sure exactly when a ship would arrive in port. Hudson's letter of invitation from the VOC instructed him to take up lodging at an inn the company directors recommended, and then inform them by letter of his arrival.

Hudson hired a wagoner to take him and his luggage to the inn. He was an experienced enough traveller to know how to tell an honest conveyor from the waterfront thieves who preyed on the unwary. Hudson was glad that his wagon driver had a stout-looking son who sat in the back of the wagon with a heavy stick to discourage any would-be robbers who might cast an eye on his property. As an added precaution, Hudson kept the waterproof oilskin bag that contained his precious charts secure on his lap. He held his trusty walking stick in clear view of anyone who might want to grab that bag and run with it. To lose a parcel of his clothing to thieves would certainly be an annoyance, but clothes could be replaced. Hudson's charts were irreplaceable. They were his life!

Hudson was relieved when the wagoner's route took them away from the waterfront. He had been concerned that the VOC might be as penny-pinching as the Muscovy Company, and lodge him in a cheap dockside inn among the seedy taverns and brothels that catered to common sailors. Hudson knew what those places were like. In the best of them you slept without blanket or pillow on a dirty floor with twenty other men who snored, broke wind, and stank of stale beer. In the worst of them you were lucky if you didn't wake up with your throat cut and your property stolen.

The Amsterdam that Hudson saw, once he got away from the waterfront, was nothing like London with its sprawling suburbs. Though it equalled London as a centre of finance and commerce, Amsterdam was more compact, only a quarter the size of the English capital. The Amsterdam canals, for which the city was famous, were certainly more picturesque than the grimy thoroughfares of London, even if they were lined with warehouses.

Best of all for Hudson, after his unpleasant crossing from England, the inn his driver took him to was in a respectable part of the city. It was a clean and comfortable hostelry. After Hudson had paid the wagoner and his son, the inn's proprietor showed him to a private room with a good bed and a small stove for heat. It had an east-facing window to let in the morning sunlight.

Hudson had met some surly innkeepers in his time, but this man treated him with friendly respect. He assured Hudson that his establishment served the best food in Amsterdam. To prove it, he sat his English guest down at a table in the kitchen and served him a hearty meal of roast pork, bread, cheese, and lager.

When Hudson laid his head on his pillow that night, he was happier than he had been in months. He fell asleep confident that in Amsterdam he would renew his career. He would get another chance at the Northwest Passage. He could not have dreamed of the intrigues that lay in wait for him.

The following morning Hudson sent a letter by messenger to East India House, the VOC's magnificent Amsterdam headquarters. To his surprise, no answer came that day. However, the following morning Hudson received a letter under the VOC seal. The author, Dirk Van Os, welcomed Hudson to Amsterdam, and encouraged him to enjoy the sights of the city. Then Van Os advised Hudson that perhaps in a week or so the directors of the VOS would be ready to meet him.

Hudson was no fool. He knew the old trick: keep a man waiting for days so that when he finally has his interview, he is so anxious to reach an agreement, he will accept almost any terms. Hudson had no intention of spending the next week as a tourist in Amsterdam. He left instructions with the innkeeper that if anyone came looking for him, they could reach him at the home of Peter Plancius in The Hague.

Peter Plancius was a Flemish-born theologian and minister in the Dutch Reformed Church. He had fled to the Netherlands to escape religious persecution. He was also one of the foremost mapmakers of his time, and was cartographer for the VOC. There is no record of how he came to be a friend of Henry Hudson, but it would not be surprising if they became acquainted through Richard Hakluyt.

Plancius welcomed Hudson to his home. Like Hakluyt, Plancius was fascinated with geography and the idea of exploring unknown parts of the world. He couldn't get enough of Hudson's stories about the Arctic, and he proudly showed Hudson charts he owned that had been made by the Dutch explorers William Barents and Jacob van Heemskerk.

The two men spent long hours discussing the northern seas and the discoveries Hudson and other explorers had made. Hudson unrolled his charts and traced what he thought could be possible routes to the Far East. Plancius saw that Hudson's eyes shone when he spoke of his desire to find the short route to Cathay. It was clear to Plancius that Hudson believed finding that route was his destiny, just as it had been Columbus' destiny to discover the New World. The man's enthusiasm was almost contagious.

Hudson told Plancius that, in his opinion, there was no Northeast Passage. The Northwest was the place to look. If the VOC would put him in command of an expedition to the Furious Overfall, Hudson said, he would find the Northwest Passage.

At this Plancius became silently thoughtful. Hudson had shown considerable trust in allowing him to see his charts. Plancius was, after all, a cartographer in the employ of the VOC, and could take unfair advantage of that trust. But Plancius, like Hakluyt, was a scholar who believed knowledge was more important than the financial rewards that were the ultimate goal of the VOC. He also valued his friendship with Hudson, whom he had begun to admire as a man with a vision.

Plancius promised Hudson that he would keep all they had discussed in confidence. He said he did not feel obliged to tell the directors of the VOC what he had seen on Hudson's charts, nor about what knowledge Hudson had of the Furious Overfall. He said that the VOC might use that information to send one of their own Dutch captains on a quest for the route to Cathay. Plancius advised Hudson to say nothing about the Furious Overfall to the VOC when he finally got his chance to speak to them. He also told Hudson not to repeat to the VOC his belief that the Northeast Passage did not exist. Instead, he should present himself as an explorer who was willing to look once again in the seas north of Russia.

Hudson found all this perplexing. He asked Plancius why he should not just state his case to the VOC for an expedition to the Furious Overfall. Plancius replied that he knew the directors personally, and knew how their minds worked. He advised Hudson to trust him, and be patient.

Hudson had been in The Hague with Plancius for a week when a message arrived from Amsterdam. The directors of the VOC wished Hudson to meet them at East India House. They requested that Peter Plancius, who had been so kind in extending his hospitality to Hudson, provide the captain with a horse.

Henry Hudson was more accustomed to the rolling deck of a ship than he was to the bounce of a horseback ride over poor roads. By the time he arrived at his Amsterdam inn he was stiff and sore. He sent a message to East India House, informing the VOC that he was back in the city.

The next morning a driver with a small carriage arrived at the inn to take Hudson to East India House in the centre of Amsterdam. Hudson was awestruck when he saw the VOC headquarters. It made the Muscovy Company's office on Budge Row in London look insignificant.

Hudson's carriage passed through a gate of Tuscan design into a small tunnel. It emerged in a large courtyard flanked by two long two-storey buildings. Hudson's driver told him that these were the VOC's principal warehouses. Stored in them, he boasted, was a fortune in spices, silks, jewels, and other exotic goods.

At the bottom of the courtyard was another imposing building that connected the two long structures. It was three storeys high, and crowned with a triangular upper section that added two smaller storeys. In that building, the driver said, were the VOC offices, as well as the company's archives and map room.

The facades of the buildings facing the courtyard were elegant, and the many windows created a light and airy effect. Hudson could tell that the VOC had gone to great expense to make East India House a symbol of its power and wealth. No one could look at the fine architecture and not be impressed. But this wealth did not come without a price in human suffering.

Even though this was Hudson's first visit to East India House, he knew all about the *zielverkoopers* — the "soul sellers," as every veteran sailor in Western Europe called them. Many professional sailors would not sign aboard VOC vessels that were bound for the Far East around Africa. The voyage was too long, discipline aboard the ships was too harsh, and the risk of exposure to tropical diseases was too great. Moreover, the economy-minded VOC purchased the cheapest low-quality supplies for their ships. The death rate for common sailors on VOC voyages to the Orient was roughly one-third, high even for those days.

Because experienced sailors generally knew better than to join its crews, the VOC employed low characters called crimps to round up men. Crimps would use any means possible to lure or drag their victims onto VOC ships. They waylaid common drunks, and scoured the poor parts of the city for men who were in such desperate straits that they would do almost anything for a few silver coins. Crimps loitered around the gates of the city, watching for naïve young men from the country. They would fill the unsuspecting youths' heads with wonderful tales of life at sea and the chances of making a fortune. The crimps even gave the young men little hammers they said they would need to bang jewels out of rocks when they reached the Orient. Crimps would actually travel to farm villages and convince parents that gold and glory awaited strong young lads willing to learn the sailor's trade. The victims wouldn't discover the terrible truth until it was too late. Once a man (or boy) had signed an agreement with a crimp, he had "sold his soul," as the saying went. The VOC owned him, almost like a slave. He was in for a brutal round trip voyage of two or three years. He received no pay until he returned to Amsterdam — if he survived. For recruiting him, the crimp received 150 guilders from the VOC, which was deducted from the victim's pay.

Knowing all this about the VOC and its dealings with the *zielverkoopers*, Hudson was under no illusion that the men he was about to meet were anything but flint-hearted businessmen. Like the directors of the Muscovy Company, they were driven solely by the desire for profit. Whatever they wanted from him, they would try to get it as cheaply as possible.

In contrast to the beautiful outer face of East India House, the room in which Hudson finally met three of the directors was rather austere. It was small, with row upon row of ledger books lining the walls. It reminded Hudson of an accountant's office. Three men dressed in the staid clothing of respectable Dutch Burghers sat on one side of a long rectangular table. Hudson thought they resembled magistrates at a tribunal court. They introduced themselves as Dirk Van Os, Isaac Le Maire, and Jan Poppe. They invited Hudson to be seated in a chair opposite them, and offered him a glass of sherry. These men spoke some English, but a company interpreter was on hand to ensure that there would be no errors in communication.

Van Os spoke first, and he wasted no time with small talk. He told Hudson that the men before him were only a committee representing the seventeen directors of the Dutch East India Company. Any decisions concerning the day's proceedings would be made by a vote involving all of the directors. Then, before Hudson could even nod in polite agreement, Van Os asked him to state his case for a short route to the Orient.

Hudson talked for almost two hours. He said that he believed a Northeast Passage could be found. He explained that his two previous voyages for the Muscovy Company had not been failures, as was commonly believed. Those expeditions, he said, had been probes into vast unknown regions, and had yielded priceless geographic information. Hudson pointed out that while he did not yet know exactly where the Northeast Passage was, he knew where it *wasn't*. That knowledge considerably narrowed the regions that still called for exploration.

Hudson produced carefully selected charts to support his theories. He argued that the northern ice pack was still a little-understood phenomenon, but that its mysteries would be solved, just as the riddles of the tides and ocean currents had been solved by navigators of an earlier age.

Le Maire asked Hudson if he had told Emanuel Van Meteran in London that he had concluded that the Northeast Passage did not exist. Hudson was prepared for this question. He had been thinking about it ever since his conversations with Plancius, because he *had* in fact told Van Meteran that very thing.

Sitting before the dour-faced VOC men, Hudson still believed that any further search for a Northeast Passage was doomed to failure. But keeping Plancius' advice in mind, Hudson was not straightforward. He said that Van Meteran had misunderstood him. The Northeast Passage was there, somewhere. He had just been looking in the wrong places.

Hudson was learning the slippery tricks of intrigue. He showed the VOC directors some of his charts, but not all of them. When they at last peppered him with questions, he answered some directly, but was evasive with others. Hudson knew that these men were trying to pick his brain. If he surrendered anything to them in an unguarded moment, they would seize it, and he would get nothing in return.

That night, while Hudson sat in his room at the inn writing a letter to Katherine, the VOC directors held a late meeting. Le Maire liked what he had seen of Henry Hudson. He had been impressed by what Hudson said, and he thought his accomplishments were admirable. Nobody, not even the Dutch hero Barents, had sailed as far north as this Englishman. Le Maire, who was Flemish, not Dutch, favoured sending Hudson off to find the Northeast Passage. A few directors agreed with him. But the majority, showing their stiff Dutch reserve, were opposed. No matter how optimistically Hudson had described things, they argued, he had in fact failed twice to find the Northeast Passage. Moreover, they strongly sensed that he had not told them everything he knew. They didn't think he was trustworthy.

One VOC director was not present at this meeting; a very powerful man named Balthazar de Moucheron. He had been against sending for Hudson in the first place. Rather than participate in the discussion, he had gone to his home in the country. His vote was nonetheless necessary for the directors' decision to be official. The next morning a messenger from East India House took a letter to de Moucheron. It outlined both sides of the dispute, and asked for his valued opinion.

De Moucheron read the letter carefully. Then he waited two days before sending his laconic reply. "Master Hudson's plans are not a good investment for the Dutch East India Company."

Van Os, Poppe, Le Maire, and the other directors knew there could be no expedition without de Moucheron's support. But they did not want to permanently cut their ties with Hudson. The Englishman knew more than he was letting on, and might yet prove useful.

Hudson had been kept waiting for days. He had all but run out of patience, and was ready to pack up his belongings and go back to London, when a messenger from East India House arrived at his inn with a letter. The directors of the VOC respectfully asked him to meet them the following morning.

Once again Hudson sat in the small room and looked across the table at Van Os, Poppe, and Le Maire. With a display of great regret, they apologized for having kept him waiting for so long. Not all of the company directors were in Amsterdam, they explained, and in spite of every effort, they had been unable to contact the absent members. Therefore, the VOC could not come to a final decision on his proposal. They said that all of their colleagues would be present for a meeting in the spring of 1609, about five months away. Perhaps they would have more promising news for him then. The directors gave Hudson enough money to cover all of his travel expenses, but offered nothing for his time.

Hudson was not surprised by the polite dismissal, nor did he consider himself defeated. He left Amsterdam that same day, but not for England. Hudson wasn't about to spend five idle months waiting for a message that might not come at all. He went straight to Peter Plancius in The Hague.

Plancius listened closely to Hudson's detailed report of all that had transpired in Amsterdam. Then he said that the time had come for them to shake the VOC up a little. They were going to very subtly bring the king of France into their intrigue.

It was no secret that the French were every bit as interested in a short route to Cathay as the English and the Dutch. Jacques Cartier had searched for a passage through the Americas, and had discovered the great St. Lawrence River. The French king, Henry IV, had supported expeditions of discovery that were slowly but surely filling in the map of the land Cartier had named Canada. But the Northwest Passage had proven just as elusive for the French as it had for their English and Dutch rivals.

What might happen, Plancius asked Hudson suggestively, if King Henry should be made aware that Europe's foremost Arctic explorer was available for hire?

Plancius knew better than to directly contact the French, which the Dutch government would consider treason. Instead, he wrote a letter to Isaac Le Maire, the one VOC director who had strongly supported Hudson. The letter hinted, in a vague fashion, that Henry Hudson had secret information about a Northwest Passage.

Le Maire took the bait. He thought he had been right about Hudson all along. But he was a director of a company that had just turned Hudson down, and he could not afford to compromise his position. There was a way around that problem.

Isaac Le Maire had a brother, Jacob, who was a navigator working for the French. Jacob was a confidant of Pierre Jeannin, one of Henry IV's closest friends and advisors. A letter, passed from one individual to another, led to a meeting in The Hague between Jacob Le Maire and Jeannin. Le Maire told Jeannin that the famous English explorer, Henry Hudson, could be available for France. The Muscovy Company had not re-hired him, and there was a rumour that the VOC had broken off negotiations with him.

Jeannin was interested, but he wanted this information confirmed by Hudson personally. A meeting was arranged. Hudson told Jeannin only that he had not yet reached an agreement with anyone regarding a new voyage of exploration. That wasn't a lie. It just wasn't the whole truth.

Jeannin, being well experienced in the intrigues of the French court, suspected that Hudson wasn't telling him everything. He went to Plancius to see if he might pry some information out of the VOC cartographer. Plancius admitted that he and Captain Hudson had been collaborating on a project.

Then Jacob Le Maire told Jeannin that if the French made a deal with Hudson, he wanted a share of any benefits that came of it. Jeannin was now convinced not only that Hudson was available, but also that the French had better secure his services before someone else did. He agreed to Jacob Le Maire's request, and then wrote a letter to King Henry, strongly advising him to sponsor a Hudson expedition.

> Plancius maintains, according to the reasons of his science, and from the information given him, both by the Englishman [Hudson] and other pilots, who have been engaged in the same navigation, that there must be in the northern parts a passage corresponding to the one found near the South Pole by Magellan ... It will be pleasing to Your Majesty's ear that Hudson believes he will soon discover a short passage to the Indies. It is said everywhere that he and Plancius stand agreed on the route he will take. The talents of these men are formidable.
>
> The whole voyage, both out and home, can be finished in six months without approaching any of the harbors or fortresses of the King of Spain; whilst by the road round the Cape of Good Hope, which is now in common use, one generally requires three years and one is besides exposed to meet and fight the Portuguese.
>
> Hudson will sail in no ship that does not meet his own requirements. That Your Majesty has many ships suitable for the purpose is a certainty. Jacob Le Maire, of whom I have already

spoken to Your Majesty in this letter, believes
that an additional sum of four thousand crowns,
in gold, must be spent to prepare a ship for such
a voyage. He does not know what wages Hudson
will require. Nor does he know whether Hudson
will sail with a French crew. Nor do I.

Jacob Le Maire asked for a signed copy of the letter to insure
his own interests, and Jeannin gave one to him. Le Maire showed
the letter to Hudson and Plancius. The two conspirators were
pleased with the way the plot was working. But Plancius had yet
another manoeuvre to make.

Hudson and Plancius differed on where the short route
to the Orient would most likely be found. Hudson argued in
favour of a Northwest Passage. Plancius still strongly believed in
a Northeast Passage. Plancius had another meeting with Jeannin.
In the course of their conversation he casually mentioned his
convictions about a Northeast Passage. He said nothing about
Hudson's obsession with the Furious Overfall. Jeannin had the
impression that Hudson wanted to make another search by way
of the North Pole. He reported that to King Henry.

Hudson remained in The Hague to await the next development in this drama of half-truths and whispered conspira-
cies. He stayed at the home of Jodocus Hondius, a friend and
fellow scholar of Hakluyt and Plancius. Hondius was Flemish.
He had lived for a while in London, where he might have first
met Hudson. He was a renowned engraver, sculptor, and metal-
worker who had engraved portraits of such celebrated English
heroes as Sir Francis Drake. Hondius was also one of the most
accomplished cartographers of his time. His maps were remark-
able not only for their accuracy, but also for their beauty. In

addition to being a navigational aid, a Hondius map was a genuine work of art.

Whether or not Hudson and Hondius had been previously acquainted, they became good friends during Hudson's stay in The Hague. Hudson provided Hondius with details of his Arctic expeditions, and assisted him in drawing a map of the Far North. That map would later be considered one of Hondius' greatest contributions to the science of geography.

Hondius evidently tried to discourage Hudson from looking for a Northwest Passage. Like Plancius, he was certain that the Northeast Passage was the key. With two of the most learned men in Western Europe prevailing upon him to give up on the idea of a Northwest Passage, Hudson might indeed have finally agreed to see things their way. Then, while he was still lodging with Hondius, Hudson received a letter and a parcel from another friend, Captain John Smith.

Smith was about ten years younger than Hudson. He was an English adventurer with a colourful past. He had been a mercenary, a merchant sailor, and a pirate. He had been captured by Turks and sold as a slave, but managed to escape. Smith was one of the founders of the Jamestown Colony in Virginia. According to legend, Smith was taken prisoner by Powhatan Natives and was about to be executed when the chief's daughter, Pocahontas, saved his life.

Smith had just returned to London from Jamestown and learned that Hudson was in The Hague. As a longtime friend, he was well aware of Hudson's desire to find the short route to Cathay. Smith had done some exploring himself, and was a skilled mapmaker. In the letter he told Hudson that he believed a passage through America to the Pacific lay to the north of Virginia. He sent Hudson some maps he had made based on information he'd been given by Natives. Smith had been told of "seas" to the north, which would later prove to be the Great Lakes. Like most of the people of that time, Smith thought that North America was only a few hundred miles wide at the most, and that the seas the Natives told him about were a single body of water joining the Atlantic and Pacific oceans. Armed with Smith's letter and charts, Hudson once again told Hondius that the short route to Cathay lay through a Northwest Passage. Hondius was happy to copy Smith's maps, and add them to his archives.

Meanwhile, Jacob Le Maire showed his brother Isaac his copy of the letter Jeannin had written to King Henry. Isaac went straight to East India House, where he put on an act worthy of a great thespian. Speaking like a man who had just received shocking news and in a highly agitated state, he told the VOC directors that he had irrefutable proof that the king of France was about to sponsor Henry Hudson's next voyage. Hudson was going to try once again to find the route to the Indies across the top of the world. Should he be successful, Paris would become the most important trading centre in Europe.

The directors were alarmed. They decided immediately that under no circumstances should they allow Hudson to sign a contract with Henry IV. It was now December 29, 1608. The VOC sent Hudson a letter by special messenger, urging him to come to Amsterdam at his earliest convenience. Hudson and Plancius could barely contain their glee when they read the letter. But they knew Hudson must not appear to be *too* anxious to go back to East India House. Now it was the VOC's turn to be kept waiting. Hudson replied that he would go to Amsterdam after he had celebrated the New Year.

Hudson went to Amsterdam early in January 1609. Hondius went with him as an interpreter. Hudson felt, with good reason, that he could not entirely trust the VOC's own interpreter. On January 8, Hudson signed a contract with the VOC. It was written in Dutch, and Hondius signed it as Hudson's witness. Dirk Van Os and Jan Poppe signed for the VOC.

The contract was specific about where Hudson was supposed to go. He was to search for a Northeast Passage north of Novaya Zemlya. Nowhere in the contract was he given permission to sail off in any direction at his own discretion. The agreement also stated:

> He [Hudson] shall obtain as much knowledge of the lands as can be done without any considerable loss of time, and if it is possible return immediately in order to make a faithful report and relation of his voyage to the Directors, and to deliver over his journals, log-books and charts, together with an account of everything whatsoever which shall happen to him during the voyage without keeping anything back.

Hudson accepted the rather modest sum of eight hundred guilders as his fee. In the event that he did not return from the voyage, the VOC would pay his wife an additional two hundred guilders. This was a bargain for the company, considering that it cost in excess of one hundred thousand guilders to send a ship around Africa to the Orient.

The terms of the contract also stated that while Hudson was away, his wife and children were to live in Amsterdam, at the expense of the VOC. This was a strange clause. Perhaps the VOC wanted Hudson's family as hostages in case he was up to some sort of trick. But as usual, John Hudson would be sailing with his father. Oliver Hudson was a married man with a family of his own. Although he signed the document, Hudson had no intention of uprooting Katherine and Richard from their comfortable home to spend a large part of the year living in Amsterdam among strangers.

In rather vague wording, the VOC promised Hudson financial rewards if his voyage should prove successful. They also required Hudson and his family to take up residence in the Netherlands when he returned, and for him to work for the VOC and no other company. That was another condition Hudson ignored.

The new expedition was scheduled to embark in early April. Hudson returned to The Hague for one more consultation with Plancius. The cartographer still held the opinion that a Northeast Passage existed. He tried to persuade Hudson to live up to the agreement he had signed with the VOC. Hudson said that he would search for a Northeast Passage, but Plancius was certain that he had other ideas.

Once again, Peter Plancius demonstrated the faith he had in Hudson as a friend and an explorer. He presented Hudson with one of his most prized possessions, the journals of the English explorer George Weymouth. If Hudson was wide-eyed and speechless at the sight of them, he had good cause. By giving him the documents, Plancius had shown that he knew perfectly well that Hudson did not intend to fully honour the terms of his contract. It also meant that Plancius was not going to report his suspicions to the directors. Moreover, the papers were of vital importance to anyone who hoped to explore the Furious Overfall.

In 1602, George Weymouth had been sponsored by the Muscovy Company and the English East India Company to investigate the Furious Overfall as a possible key to the Northwest Passage. He had carried with him a letter from Queen Elizabeth I that he hoped to hand deliver to the emperor of China. Weymouth claimed to have sailed three hundred nautical miles into the strait before ice forced him to turn back.

Even though Weymouth had failed to get through the Furious Overfall, his journals contained detailed information on shorelines and sea conditions that was priceless to a man like Hudson. And there was more. In 1605, Weymouth had explored part of the coast of what is now New England, and his journal noted that he had seen a river mouth that could be the entrance to a channel to the Pacific. En route to London, Hudson read the journals. When he arrived home he immediately wrote to Plancius, "The notes that you placed in my safekeeping are worth more than gold and silver."

Hudson's stay in London, after his lengthy business trip to the Netherlands, was brief. Katherine was not happy with the fee he had accepted. Hudson said he was fortunate to have an expedition at all, but after this one, there would be more lucrative offers for his services. Meanwhile, Hudson had to recruit the men who would be his officers on the voyage.

5

Secrets and a Sacred Oath

Why Henry Hudson sought out Robert Juet to serve as first mate remains a mystery — but that's exactly what he did. Understandably, though Hudson would have a largely Dutch crew, he would want English officers. Still, Juet had already shown himself to be temperamental and disloyal. Perhaps Juet's seamanship was of such high quality that Hudson was willing to overlook his personal flaws. Or perhaps as first mate Juet could maintain a level of discipline among the crew that Hudson could not.

The next man Hudson recruited was John Colman, whom he had promoted to mate on his first voyage. Colman had spent the past year whaling and had made a lot of money at it. However, Hudson was offering top wages; that was one of the conditions Hudson had managed to squeeze out of the tight-fisted VOC directors. Hudson took Colman on as second mate. Colman and

Juet were the only members of the crew to whom Hudson disclosed his true intentions at the very start.

Hudson apparently hired several English sailors. No list showing how many or what their names were has survived. He then returned to Amsterdam with Juet, Colman, the English seamen, and his son John.

In Amsterdam, Hudson found that the VOC had hired some Dutch sailors, including a bo'sun, bringing the total crew number to about sixteen. Colman did not like the look of the Dutch mariners. He wrote to his wife, "I hope that these square-faced men know the sea. Looking at their fat bellies, I fear they think more highly of eating than of sailing." Juet was also unimpressed with the Dutch sailors. "They are an ugly lot," he wrote in his journal.

Although the names of the Dutch mariners are not known, they were evidently veterans of the round-Africa route to India. They might also have had some experience as "sea-beggars," the Dutch equivalent of the English seadogs. The sea-beggars had gained considerable notoriety by raiding Spanish shipping. No doubt Hudson's Dutch crewmen were a rough bunch, but they were used to sailing tropical waters, not the frigid seas that he was taking them to. Hudson thought that might suit his purposes admirably.

There were problems almost as soon as Hudson and his company arrived in Amsterdam. For some unknown reason Hudson quarreled with a VOC official named Dirck Gerritsz. Then he had to deal with representatives of the VOC's Zeeland office. These men had been against the project in the first place, and now they objected to the high wages that were to be paid to the Englishmen. In a fit of temper, Hudson stormed away from the meeting, telling the Dutchmen they could find another captain.

The Zeeland directors wrote to the Amsterdam directors, "We are much surprised at Mr. Hudson's strange behaviour and consider it inadvisable to let him undertake the voyage, for if he begins to rebel here under our eyes what will he do if he is away from us?" The Zeeland office recommended

> [T]hat wheras the said Hutson [*sic*] has taken his departure he shall remain dismissed; and even if he came to change his mind with respect to performing the journey Your Honours shall in no wise engage him but leave him dismissed. And whereas there was advanced to him certain monies to the amount of twenty-five pounds more or less, Your Honours shall compel the said Hutson, by law or arrest, to repay the aforesaid monies which the Company has advanced him.

The letter went on to say that Peter Plancius should find a "competent and sensible person" to replace Hudson as commander of the expedition.

However, it was early March when this clash took place. That didn't leave much time for finding a captain to replace Hudson, much less one who had his experience and knowledge of Arctic seas. Hudson probably knew that when he walked away. He also knew that the Amsterdam directors dominated the decision making of the VOC, and would ignore any complaints from the Zeeland office, which they did. Hudson returned to making preparations for the voyage. However, the Amsterdam members added another clause to the contract, strictly forbidding Hudson, "To think of discovering no other route or passage, except the route around the north or northeast, above Nova Zembla ... If it could

not be accomplished at the time, another route would be the subject of consideration for another voyage." In short, Hudson was
absolutely forbidden to go searching for a Northwest Passage!

Hudson had thought that the VOC would provide him with
one of its newer, larger vessels for this expedition. He was therefore disappointed when he was told he was getting the *Half Moon*,
which was not large and possibly not new. Records indicate that
the *Half Moon* was built in 1608. But she might have been older,
and may have been chosen by the VOC to offset some of the
expedition's other costs, such as the English mariners' wages. It
is interesting to note the ship's name, because the Dutch sea-
beggars wore a half moon medallion as a good luck talisman.

The *Half Moon* was a three-masted, square-rigged, flat-
bottomed *jaght* (yacht) of just sixty tons; what the English
called a flyboat. She was eighty-five feet in length, and a little

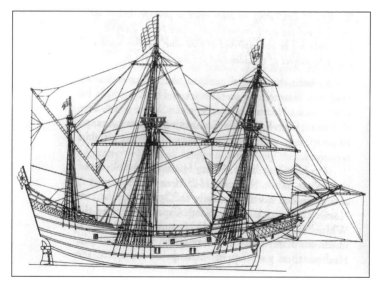

Drawing of the rig and sail plan for a reproduction of the Half Moon.

over seventeen feet in the beam. Her poopdeck and forecastle (fo'c'sle) rose higher than those on English ships of the same size. At first sight of the ship, Hudson thought she looked clumsy and rode too high in the water. He wrote to Isaac Le Maire, "I fear that she will prove difficult to handle in rough weather."

No doubt Hudson took great pride in the skills of English shipbuilders. However, at that time the Dutch were constructing ships that were faster and more manoeuvrable than the heavier English vessels. Because of their flat bottoms, they had more cargo space than was evident at first glance. No blueprint remains of the *Half Moon*, because none was used. The Dutch had developed a method of ship construction called the tangent arc system that a good shipwright could easily memorize. Once he had learned the system, the shipwright did not need a blueprint. That meant there were no plans on paper or parchment that spies could steal. Like most Dutch ships the *Half Moon* was colourfully painted.

Hudson wanted a bigger ship. Now it was the VOC's turn to present an ultimatum. Dirk Van Os, with impatience clearly showing in his words, sent Hudson a short note.

> The *Half Moon* is the only ship at the disposal of the Dutch East India Company. If you read your contract again, you will see that we are living up to our bargain. We can give you no other ship. If you do not want the *Half Moon*, the Company will be obliged to find another Captain to carry out this assignment.

Hudson knew that it was highly unlikely the VOC could find another qualified captain at this late date. But he decided not to push the issue. He would make do with the *Half Moon*. However, that did not end the petty bickering.

The officers' quarters aboard the *Half Moon* were tiny. Hudson had his own cabin, but there was no room in it for a private galley. Hudson, therefore, had one of the mates' cabins converted to a captain's galley. He was entirely within his rights to do this, as the captain was expected to take his meals separately from the crew. But this meant that the first and second mates had to share a cabin, and Juet was not a man who liked an intrusion into his privacy.

There were differences between the Dutch and English crewmen. They did not speak each others' languages, and apparently made no efforts to develop friendships. The English sailors were not at all happy when they saw that the *Half Moon*'s provisions included many barrels of salted herring, but very little beef. To the English seamen, salted or pickled beef was a staple. Herring, or any other kind of fish, was only served to provide a little variety in shipboard fare. Dutch sailors, on the other hand, were content with a daily diet of fish, and that suited the VOC because in the Netherlands beef was expensive.

To satisfy his English crewmen, Hudson requested that the VOC provide him with funds to purchase pickled beef. Growing ever more exasperated at how difficult (in their minds) Hudson was proving to be, the directors refused the request. If salted herring was good enough for Dutchmen, it was good enough for Englishmen!

Hudson believed he knew what was best for his men. He went to an Amsterdam beef merchant himself, and purchased enough barrels of pickled beef to keep his English sailors happy. He had the bill sent to Dirk Van Os. By the time Van Os learned of this, the pickled beef was stowed away in the *Half Moon*'s hold.

The outraged director ranted that Hudson had no authority to make such purchases. Hudson ignored the complaint and Van Os paid the bill.

Then the English sailors grumbled when they learned that the ship's cook would be a Dutchman. There was good reason for the men to be concerned about this. To a great degree, the cook contributed to the harmony — or lack of it — aboard ship during a long voyage. Mealtime was one of the few pleasurable moments in a sailor's working day, and well-fed men were less likely to grumble and quarrel. Some dishonest cooks would purchase only the cheapest, poorest quality provisions for the crew, and pocket the money they saved. These cooks were contemptuously called "belly-robbers." A good cook did his best with the limited menu at his disposal to serve the men properly prepared, hearty meals. He could make almost anything taste good. A good cook knew how to combine such simple ingredients as salt meat, onions, and crumbled biscuits to make a dish the sailors liked. However, a bad cook turned out unappetizing swill that sailors ate only because they were hungry. A bad cook's food would be full of "galley pepper" (ashes from the fire). He would use a lot of salt as a substitute for actual flavour, and he might even snare a few rats in the hold to add extra meat to a stew.

In the case of Hudson's crew, the English sailors did not like the idea of having a "foreign" cook. Second mate Colman wrote to his wife of the apprehension felt even by the ship's officers: "Men have been known to die of slow poisoning at sea when fed by a foreign cook." The English had their own ways of preparing food, and trusted no others.

Hudson could not send to England for another cook, and even if he did, no doubt there would be objections from the Dutch members of the crew. Instead, he decided to personally demonstrate to his English sailors that there was nothing wrong with the Dutch cook's food. About ten days before the *Half Moon* was scheduled to sail, Hudson went aboard and had the cook prepare his supper. Robert Juet recorded Hudson's opinion of the meal in his journal. "The Captain swears that he has never tasted finer edibles." Then, true to his suspicious nature, Juet added, "I wonder if he tells the truth."

Hudson was concerned about how his Dutch-built ship would stand up to the rigours of Arctic sailing, so he ordered his men to test all of the sails and rigging, as well as every coil of rope. Everything seemed up to his high standards, but Hudson wanted to be prepared for any problem that might arise. He told the VOC that he wanted spares; extra sails and yardarms.

The directors were dumbfounded at the Englishman's gall. After all the clashes they'd had with Hudson over expenses, here he was presenting them with yet another costly demand! They replied that he could have all of the spares he wanted — if he paid for them out of his own pocket. One again Hudson took it upon himself to purchase the sails and other items from an Amsterdam merchant, and charge it all to the VOC. Dirk Van Os was so furious that when Peter Plancius held a dinner in Hudson's honour, he refused the invitation. He and some of the other men of East India House wished they had taken the advice of Balthazar de Moucheron, and sent Henry Hudson home to England.

Rumours about the difficulties the VOC was having with Hudson became the gossip of Dutch ports, and were soon carried to England. In London dockside taverns, men laid wagers as to whether or not the *Half Moon* would sail at all. Mariners who knew Hudson questioned his ability to maintain discipline on a ship that had so many "foreigners" in the crew. The general feeling was that the voyage would result in nothing but trouble.

VOC spies on both sides of the water kept their ears open, and soon began picking up threads of whispered information that supposedly originated with members of the *Half Moon*'s crew. It was news that, if true, would not be at all pleasing to the men of East India House.

Meanwhile, the VOC directors were anxious for Hudson to weigh anchor and embark. It was still March, but the Dutchmen argued that by getting an early start, Hudson would have a much better chance of finding the Northeast Passage because he would have more time to explore. No doubt that argument held some truth, but quite likely Hudson's employers also were anxious to get him out of Amsterdam before he ran up any more expenses.

Hudson said it was too early in the season to sail north. He explained that the northern seas would be full of "islands of ice." Sailing amongst them at that time of year when they would be most numerous would unnecessarily endanger the ship and crew. Van Os dismissed this sensible response, and told Hudson in a strongly worded letter that the East India Company expected him to be under way "no later than the fifteenth day of March."

Hudson was tempted to reply with an equally forceful letter, telling Van Os that as captain he had a responsibility to his crew as well as to the company, and that he knew better than men who had never laid eyes on the northern ice, what sailing conditions were like in the polar seas. But perhaps because he had been influenced by the example of Peter Plancius, Hudson decided against such direct defiance. Instead, he used his wiles.

Hudson politely agreed to the order to sail by the fifteenth. Then, to the chagrin of the VOC, from one maddening day to the next he kept finding excuses to stay in port. These were unforeseen, last minute problems, he told the directors; things that were beyond his control. The directors could only fume. It wasn't as though they could force Hudson to embark at gunpoint, as much as some of them would have liked to.

Finally, April arrived. The warm breezes of a Dutch spring blew across Amsterdam and its harbour. They apparently carried away all of the middling problems that had kept the *Half Moon* from sailing. Hudson sent his Dutch bo'sun to round up any of the crew who were not already aboard. He intended to embark that very day. Hudson was about to dash off a message advising the VOC directors that he was ready to haul anchor, when to his surprise a messenger arrived with a note demanding his immediate presence at East India House. Hudson was annoyed. After so many days of purposely delaying his departure, he was now impatient to be on his way.

In the now familiar VOC office Hudson found Van Os and a committee of his fellow businessmen in an angry mood. Van Os got straight to the point. He said that he and his colleagues had information from certain reliable sources that Hudson had no intention of searching for a Northeast Passage. Instead, Van Os said accusingly, pointing a finger directly at the captain, Hudson planned to sail to the *west*! Was that or was that not true, Van Os demanded to know.

Hudson cursed himself for not sailing one day earlier. He wondered who had been talking. The few men to whom he'd said anything about his plans had been sworn to secrecy. Had somebody run off at the mouth after too much Dutch lager?

With a great show of indignation, Hudson denied Van Os's charges. Wherever did they hear such nonsense? He had signed his own good name to a contract stating that he would search for a Northeast Passage!

Van Os was not convinced. He told Hudson that the *Half Moon* was to remain in port while the VOC considered the situation. The directors did not trust Hudson to take the vessel out of their sight. Van Os warned the captain of severe legal consequences if he should be caught attempting to sail without their permission. The harbour authorities had been alerted, and would be watching.

Hudson returned to his lodging in a foul temper. He summoned Juet and Colman, and asked if either of them had said anything to anyone about his plans. Colman said he had not, but admitted to having heard some waterfront gossip. He said he did not know how the rumours had started, but he swore they had not begun with him. Juet insisted that he had not said a word to a soul, and that he hadn't even heard the rumours. Hudson believed Colman. He wasn't sure about Juet.

Two days passed. In that time Hudson did not go near the *Half Moon*. He didn't want to give the VOC spies who he knew were watching him anything to report. He wrote letters, studied his charts, and waited. Finally, Hudson was called back to East India House.

There, in the presence of several directors, Dirk Van Os presented Hudson with a bible. He told Hudson to put his right hand on the book and swear an oath that he would search for a Northeast Passage. Hudson was stunned!

By demanding that he swear an oath on the bible, the directors were clearly showing that they did not trust the word of Henry Hudson as a gentleman. It was an insult to his personal honour, but Hudson had no choice but to bear with it. He could not deny to himself that he had not been completely honest with the directors. But they were only merchants, interested in nothing but making money. He was a man about to undertake a mission of discovery. No oath, however sacred, was going to stand in his way.

Hudson swore on the bible. For a man steeped in the Christian faith, as Hudson and most of his contemporaries were, the oath was even more binding than a signature on a contract. But most likely the directors would have wanted further guarantees that Hudson would do what he had promised. They almost certainly assigned a man to the *Half Moon* as supercargo. This person, whose identity has been lost, was not technically a member of the crew. He was a representative of the VOC who was on board strictly to watch over the financial interests of the Dutch East India Company. Hudson would have welcomed the man into the ship's company with the respect he was due, while quietly planning to deal with him when the time came.

6

The Voyage of the Half Moon

The *Half Moon* sailed from Amsterdam on April 6, 1609. There was no farewell ceremony at the dock. The VOC directors, thoroughly displeased with Hudson, did not go down to the harbour to see him off. Nor were Hudson's two best friends in the Netherlands there to wish him luck and a safe journey. In a letter dated April 8, Jodocus Hondius wrote to Peter Plancius, "I have heard that Hudson began his adventure two days ago."

Little of Hudson's log from that epic journey has survived. Most of what is known about the voyage of the *Half Moon* comes from a journal kept by Robert Juet. It is interesting to note that Juet's journal has the *Half Moon* setting sail on March 25, "by the old account." Later he shifts over to *stilo novo*; the "new style." Western Europe was in the process of changing from the old Julian calendar, which had been in use since the time of Julius Caesar, to the more accurate Gregorian calendar, which had been adopted by Pope Gregory XIII in 1582. In 1609, England had still not accepted the Gregorian calendar.

The voyage began badly. As the *Half Moon* sailed into the North Atlantic from the Zuider Zee, a major storm swept down from the northwest. Even the most experienced sailors sometimes needed a day or two at sea to "get their sea-legs" after being ashore for an extended period of time. The crew of the *Half Moon* had not been granted this luxury, and as the ship pitched and rolled, many of them were so overcome with seasickness that they could not perform their duties. Juet noted, almost gloatingly, that young John Hudson was very frightened during the storm.

Just as Hudson had predicted, the *Half Moon* did not perform well in bad weather. But Hudson was a veteran mariner, and it did not take him long to get the feel of his ship so that he knew how to handle her in rough seas. The nor'wester howled throughout the afternoon and well into the night. With his feet planted firmly on the quarterdeck, and one hand grasping the rail, Hudson shouted orders and kept his vessel on course. The Dutch bo'sun evidently spoke some English, because the Dutch crew members seemed to have no problem responding to Hudson's instructions. Hudson remained at his post until dawn, when the weather finally began to clear.

This brought about one of the first positive signs on a voyage that had begun so inauspiciously. It did both the English and Dutch sailors good to see that they had a captain who not only knew how to guide a ship through a storm, but would also stay out on deck and endure the worst of it with his men. Hudson noted, "My men now act as though they had been sailing together for many years."

Hudson might have initially intended to sail directly west across the Atlantic. But now he was bound by his oath to sail north and fulfill the terms of his contract. Whatever his plans were beyond that, he kept them to himself. He did not even share his thoughts with John, in case someone tried to trick the boy into revealing information.

Contrary winds made the going slow, and it was a full month before Hudson sighted Norway's North Cape. Though it was the first week of May, the weather was fiercely cold. Ice formed in the rigging, making the work of the men who had to go aloft very unpleasant. Over the next two weeks, as the *Half Moon* continued north and then turned east toward Novaya Zemlya, it became clear to Hudson that his Dutch sailors were both physically and psychologically unfit for Arctic travel. Accustomed to sailing in tropical waters, the Dutchmen suffered from the cold more than their English shipmates. They were miserable, and they made no attempt to hide it. The harmony that Hudson had noted after the first storm vanished like mist before a stiff wind.

The *Half Moon*'s company divided into two hostile camps, English and Dutch. The Dutch sailors, hating the cold, tried to avoid duties that required them to go out on deck or up into the frozen rigging. They preferred to stay below decks where it was warmer, especially in the galley where the Dutch cook kept the stove hot. That left the burden of outdoor duties with the English sailors, and they resented it. While the Dutchmen complained about the cold and warmed themselves below decks, the Englishmen put in extra hours dealing with ice, snow, and frigid temperatures.

Hudson could have been firm with the Dutch sailors and ordered them to do their fair share of the work. He was the ship's master, and therefore was to be obeyed. Sailors were common labourers, and were expected to do what they were told under any circumstances. Almost any other ship's captain of that time would have stormed into the galley, barked a few orders, and sent the Dutch sailors scurrying for the decks and the rigging, fearful of a lashing if they didn't obey smartly. Hudson did not do that. Perhaps it was because he was not a strong commander. Or maybe it was because a gang of unhappy Dutch sailors suited his plans.

The English sailors lost all patience with their Dutch shipmates. They complained to Juet and Colman that the Dutch sailors were lazy and irresponsible. The mates passed the complaints on to Hudson, who then called the bo'sun into his cabin. The bo'sun defended his countrymen. He said the Dutch sailors could not be expected to work in the cold like Englishmen, who were used to a chilly, wet climate. After listening to both sides, Hudson did nothing.

The situation worsened. Angry words gave way to fistfights. Colman prudently sneaked into the crew's sleeping quarters while the men were eating in the galley, and confiscated their knives. With his vessel in the grip of near-anarchy, Hudson lectured the men on the virtues of tolerance and understanding. Another ship's master might have put an end to the trouble with strict disciplinary action.

May 19 dawned cloudy and cold, and an icy wind drove snow across the *Half Moon*'s decks. At about noon, however, the skies cleared, and Juet recorded, "we observed the sun having a slake." Just what Juet meant by that has puzzled historians for over four hundred years. In northern England, *slake* was a slang expression for an accumulation of mud or slime. Some people have therefore concluded that the crew of the *Half Moon* saw a sunspot. If so, the entry in Juet's journal would be the first recorded incident of the phenomenon. But any observer on the ship would have had to have looked at the sun with the naked eye, which would have resulted in damage to the retina. There were no telescopes on the

Half Moon. Hans Lippershey, a Dutch optician, had invented the telescope only the year before, and that year (1609) the Italian scientist Galileo Galilei made the first working model. Before that, a person might have been able to see a sunspot at dawn or dusk, when the sun appears large and the glare is filtered by atmosphere, but Juet put the sighting at high noon, when it would be almost impossible for the naked eye to see something as small as a sunspot. Those who dispute the sunspot theory believe that unusual cloud conditions caused an optical illusion known as a solar halo, and that was the *slake* of which Juet wrote. Whatever the men saw in the sky that day, it was not a sight that was familiar to them, and was quite likely unnerving to superstitious sailors.

By now the *Half Moon* was approaching Novaya Zemlya. As on his previous expedition, Hudson saw that any possible route through or around the island barrier was blocked by ice. He had fulfilled the terms of his contract and he had lived up to his oath. He had looked for a Northeast Passage. He could not be blamed if the passage was not there.

What happened next aboard the *Half Moon* is not clear. Either Hudson presented the crew with a new plan of action entirely of his own free will, or the crew threatened mutiny and forced Hudson to plot a course that would take them out of the polar seas. Juet's journal is so vague at this point, that some historians have speculated that he may well have instigated a mutiny, but did not write about it, as that could have incriminated him.

If there was in fact a threat of mutiny, it suited Hudson's plans admirably, especially if he had a VOC agent aboard, recording everything for his masters in Amsterdam. Whether he acted voluntarily or was in a situation in which it at least appeared that his hand was forced, Hudson offered the men choices. He said it was evident that there was no Northeast Passage, and they would have to leave the Arctic. He would not force the men to endure the cold any more than was absolutely necessary. Hudson told the men they had the option of returning to Amsterdam, but if they did that they would be regarded as failures. His own reputation would be ruined. Moreover, if the crew had threatened mutiny he would be obliged to report them as mutineers, and they would have to suffer the consequences at the hands of Dutch authorities. Dutch courts were just as harsh with mutineers as English courts were. They hanged them!

Then Hudson presented an alternative. He told the men they could retain their good names and their self-esteem by crossing the Atlantic and searching for a Northwest Passage. They might even earn everlasting glory, not to mention a rich financial reward, by finding it.

Hudson told the men he had been studying the evidence for years, and he had good reason to believe there were two possible gateways to the Northwest Passage. One was the Furious Overfall. None of the *Half Moon*'s crew had heard of this deadly strait, so they were not aware that it lay in the Arctic. The other, Hudson said, was a river mouth that was somewhere between the English colony of Virginia and the mouth of the St. Lawrence River. He told the crew that he had learned of this second possibility from none other than his friend Captain John Smith, a man whose name the English sailors knew well.

Hudson left it up to the crew to decide whether they should sail to Amsterdam or the New World. It didn't take them long to see the wisdom of sailing west, instead of returning to the Netherlands with nothing. Hudson would have prevailed upon the VOC agent to give his official permission for the westward expedition, as the representative of the Dutch East India Company. Otherwise, Hudson would have been technically guilty of stealing the *Half Moon* for his own purposes; in short, piracy! There was one decision that Hudson insisted must be left to him alone. When they had crossed the Atlantic, he would decide whether they would set their course for the Furious Overfall or for Captain Smith's river. The crew had to agree that whatever course Hudson chose, they would abide by it.

With his crew solidly behind him, Henry Hudson made the most historically dramatic U-turn in the annals of exploration. Dutch and English sailors once again worked happily side by side as they left Novaya Zemlya and its forbidding ice packs in the *Half Moon*'s wake. It was fortunate indeed that Hudson restored peace among the crewmen when he did, because a few days later a monstrous storm roared down from the north, and every hand was needed to prevent the *Half Moon* from foundering.

The lookout in the crow's nest had just sighted the Lofoten Islands when the heavy winds struck and the seas rose in mountains of green water. The lookout was fortunate to avoid being blown overboard as he clambered down to the main deck. Hudson realized within minutes that he and his men faced a life-and-death battle with a storm they would tell their grandchildren about — if they survived.

Hudson shouted to Juet to join him on the quarterdeck, and then told him to remain there no matter what happened. There was a grim purpose to that order. If anything happened to the captain, the first mate would be in a position to take immediate command.

Hudson then called for all sails to be taken in. With her canvass fully spread from the yardarms, the *Half Moon* was a toy for the wind to blow whichever way it pleased. If the spars and masts were naked, the ship would bob like a cork on the water, but would be less likely to capsize.

Every man on the *Half Moon* knew this. But looking up at the swaying masts and at yardarms that almost dipped in the sea as the ship rolled from side to side, they were paralyzed with fear. It was all a man could do to cling to the rail to keep from being washed overboard. How could the captain expect anyone to go aloft and haul in sails?

The answer came from second mate John Colman and the captain's teenaged son. At the height of the storm Colman and John Hudson risked their lives and put their shipmates to shame when they climbed the rigging and began to haul in the topsail. Hudson watched with even measures of pride and anxiety while his son clung to the yardarm as he rolled up the canvas. If the boy had been afraid in that earlier storm, he had overcome his fear and was doing a man's part now. One slip on that yardarm and he'd fall straight into the raging sea. There would be no chance of rescue.

Hudson bellowed at the crewmen, asking them if they were afraid to go where a boy had gone. Neither the English nor the Dutch sailors wanted the other group to take them for cowards. Cursing the storm and the sea, they scrambled up the rigging. Soon all of the *Half Moon*'s sails were furled and tied. Juet wrote in his journal, "So for 24 hours we ran before the wind a distance of 210 miles."

On the afternoon of May 28, the *Half Moon* came in sight of the Faeroe Islands, a rocky, windswept archipelago in the Norwegian Sea halfway between Scotland and Iceland. Hudson saw that his chart had the islands located forty-two miles too far to the west, so he made the necessary correction. He wanted to put in at one of the little ports to take on food and fresh water, but heavy seas prevented him from entering any of the harbours in the small outer islands.

Hudson could have bypassed the Faeroe Islands, but he was well aware of the fickle nature of his crew. The men had not set foot on land since leaving Amsterdam, and they had an ocean crossing ahead of them. They were restless, and they needed a break from the ship, even if it was a very brief one. Hudson ordered a sea anchor to be cast out so the ship would drift slowly through the island chain while he awaited calmer weather. This tactic worked, and on May 30, the sea was calm enough for the *Half Moon* to approach Stromo, one of the larger islands.

The inhabitants of Stromo lived by fishing, farming, and herding sheep. Generally, they were peaceful people. But they were also descendants of Vikings, and even spoke an ancient Norse dialect. They had been known to swarm aboard visiting foreign ships and hold the vessels for ransom until they were paid off in practical merchandise like cloth, as well as guns, powder, and shot. Hudson was aware of this, so he anchored the *Half Moon* in the outer part of Stromo's harbour. The local people could not possibly approach the ship without alerting the crew.

Hudson put Juet in charge of a landing party that rowed ashore to fill water casks. For the islanders, a visit from a foreign ship was always an event. Every man, woman, and child in the village turned out to look at the strangers. They wore sealskin boots and were wrapped in shaggy sheepskin cloaks. The men had bushy beards. To Juet and his men, these people looked like savages. But as uncomfortable as the Dutch and English sailors were, the islanders did nothing that could be considered threatening. Juet supervised two shore parties that day, and there was no trouble at all. By ten o'clock at night the *Half Moon*'s casks were brimming with fresh spring water.

The next morning Hudson decided to go ashore himself. He didn't trust the islanders, so he strapped on his sword and tucked a pair of pistols into his belt. He didn't think he would have to use the weapons, but he believed a show of arms would prevent trouble.

To the delight of the men, Hudson took almost the whole ship's company ashore with him, leaving only a couple of watchmen on the *Half Moon*. The mariners made a brief tour of the village, and Hudson later wrote in his journal,

> The houses of the Faeroe Islanders are the strangest I have ever seen. They are tiny huts with roofs of grass. At this season the grass is new and still green. The houses are built so near to each other that we had to walk past them in single file.

A large group of island men armed with clubs and agricultural tools followed Hudson's party at a distance. Evidently they were afraid that the strangers might steal some of their sheep. They became friendly, however, when Hudson indicated that he wanted to barter. Hudson traded eight steel knives for some green vegetables, two sacks of barley, and six sheep that were slaughtered and butchered on the spot. Then he and his men returned to the *Half Moon* and hoisted anchor.

For two weeks the men enjoyed beautiful weather and calm seas. Hudson was looking for a place marked on his chart as Busse Island. Juet noted that they were unable to find this island. Busse Island did not exist, even though explorers dating back to Martin Frobisher had reported seeing it. It's possible that those men had seen a *fata morgana*; a marine optical illusion.

Then on June 15, a violent storm whipped up almost the entire Atlantic from the equator to the Arctic Circle. For four days and nights the *Half Moon* was a toy in the jaws of the shrieking gale. Hudson was on the quarterdeck almost continually, shouting himself hoarse as he kept his terrified men moving so that they didn't have time to give up to despair. Juet wrote, "We had a great storm which broke our foremast. We lost it overboard, along with the forsesail which was set low … By reason of the unconstant weather we were forced to lie-a-trie with our mainsail."

To "lie-a-trie" meant to reduce the sails to a minimum and sail close to the wind (directly into the wind). This procedure helped ease a ship through a storm. Besides losing her foremast in this gale, the *Half Moon* also had damage to her bow. When at last the storm blew itself out on June 19, Hudson put the men to work doing repairs. When everything was shipshape again, Hudson treated the men to tots of brandywine from his personal stock.

On June 25, an event occurred that could well indicate what sort of activities Henry Hudson engaged in early in his career as a mariner. Just before noon the lookout spotted a small ship heading east. The *Half Moon* abruptly swung about and began to chase the other vessel because, as Hudson wrote in his log, "I desired to speak with her." More likely, Hudson saw an opportunity to engage in a little piracy. What better way to win the loyalty of his men than by giving them a chance at some loot!

Like most ships of that time, the *Half Moon* was armed. She had two port cannon, two starboard cannon, and two stern chasers; guns mounted on the stern where they could be fired at an enemy ship in pursuit. As the *Half Moon* closed in, the other ship put on more canvas, clearly intending to make a run for it. Hudson was flying his Dutch pennant. The other ship flew no colours. Hudson had the Dutch flag lowered and hoisted an English one. Still there was no response from the other ship. To Hudson and his men that meant that she was neither Dutch nor English, and therefore fair game.

The *Half Moon* was almost within hailing distance of the fleeing ship when at last she hoisted her colours; French! At that time England was at peace with France, so Hudson could not claim to be acting as a privateer. This would be high seas robbery, plain and simple. However, a sudden shift in the wind favoured the would-be prey. The small ship began to pull away from the *Half Moon*. After six hours, Hudson gave up the chase. He unhappily noted in his log that he had lost twelve hours of sailing time, "through no fault of mine or lack of diligence in my men."

On July 1, Hudson believed he was nearing Newfoundland. At that time the name "Newfoundland" was not necessarily limited to the large island that now makes up part of the province of Newfoundland and Labrador. It was common for mariners to call all of what is now Atlantic Canada the "new found land." Quite likely, Hudson was actually off the coast of Nova Scotia.

Hudson was aware of the rich fishing grounds here. He decided to take advantage of the opportunity to add to his ship's food supply, as well as salt down some fish to take back to Amsterdam. There was nothing better than a profitable commodity to soothe the anger of men like the VOC directors.

On July 3, the *Half Moon* approached a fleet of twelve fishing boats flying the French colours. Hudson hailed the French commander. At first the two captains exchanged polite greetings, but when Hudson indicated that he intended to fish there, the Frenchman curtly told him that he was in French waters. Hudson knew very well that the fishing grounds were not "owned" by France or anyone else. Fishing fleets from every maritime nation in Western Europe came here. But Hudson didn't want trouble. Following the advice of one of his Dutch sailors who was a veteran fisherman, Hudson moved to a location farther south where both cod and herring were running.

In a matter of just a few hours the men pulled in 118 "great cods," as Juet called them. After supper they caught another dozen. Some of the men went out in the ship's boat with nets, and hauled in so many herring that there wasn't enough salt on board to preserve them all. Hudson allowed the Dutch sailors to gorge themselves on fresh herring, which was a great favourite with them. However, the Dutchmen grumbled when Hudson said that only cod was to be salted for preservation, because cod fetched a better price in the European markets than herring did. To keep the herring alive until the cook was ready to use them, the fish were simply left in the net, which was towed behind the *Half Moon*.

Over the next few days, Hudson sailed down the coast of Nova Scotia, then turned west and skirted the entrance to the Bay of Fundy. This is one of the foggiest places in the world, and Juet had good reason to note "Very thick and misty weather" in his journal. That Hudson had turned in this direction, instead of going north to follow the coast of Labrador toward the Furious Overfall, shows that he had made up his mind to look for Captain John Smith's river. He had decided, sensibly, that in spite of whatever promises had been made, he could not trust this crew not to mutiny if he took them back into Arctic waters.

On July 12, the *Half Moon* anchored in a small cove on the coast of what is now the state of Maine. The exact location is not certain, but it was probably in Penobscot Bay. The men could see a beach of white sand backed by dense forest. Hudson was about to send Juet out with a shore party, when a blanket of thick fog suddenly rolled in. The men still wanted to go ashore, but Hudson forbade it. He did not know if this country was inhabited, and he had heard stories about the savage "Red Indians," who some accounts claimed were cannibals. He did not want anyone going ashore until the fog lifted.

For a few days the *Half Moon* tacked cautiously along the coast, with Juet making soundings as they went. The fog continued almost without interruption. Not even the English sailors could recall ever having experienced such foggy conditions. At night the ship would lay at anchor because of the danger of running onto a shoal in the darkness. With nothing else to pass the time, the men tried their hands at fishing again. Juet recorded that he alone caught fifteen cod, "some of the greatest I have seen."

On the morning of July 17, the *Half Moon* was anchored near a group of five offshore islands. A heavy fog still hung over the coast. At about ten o'clock the men heard the sounds of voices and paddles from somewhere out in the mist. When he realized the sounds were getting closer, Hudson ordered Juet to arm the men with muskets and prepare to repel boarders. He sent John to his cabin to fetch his sword and pistols.

For some tense moments the men waited, straining to pick up any sort of a warning sound from out in the grey murk. They heard voices speaking in a language that was completely alien to them. Everyone knew that fog sometimes plays tricks with sound, so the men couldn't even be certain of the exact direction the voices were coming from.

Then two long shapes emerged from the fog and drew up alongside the *Half Moon*. Hudson quickly shouted an order that no one was to shoot unless he gave the command. Looking over the side, he saw two birchbark canoes. In each were three Native men. These people, whom Hudson and Juet would both describe in their journals as "savages," had their heads plucked clean of hair except for scalplocks, and wore nothing but loincloths made from animal skins. Their leader, who spoke some broken French, greeted Hudson in a friendly manner. Hudson saw that

Rendering of the Half Moon *at anchor as Natives approach.*

the Natives were armed with nothing but stone knives, and so allowed them to climb aboard.

Hudson had some cheap trade goods on board, so he selected a few items as presents for his Native visitors. The six men accepted the blankets, beads, and mirrors Hudson gave them as though the gifts were their rightful due. Evidently they were accustomed to receiving such presents from French traders or fishermen.

Hudson told the cook to bring out food for the Natives. They wolfed down the servings of cooked herring, but refused offerings of hardtack biscuit with such a display of disgust that it was obvious they had sampled this staple of European sailors' diet before. Hardtack was as solid as iron, and definitely an acquired taste.

In his halting French, the Native leader told Hudson that not far away were large deposits of gold, silver, and copper. He said he knew of a place that was rich with diamonds, rubies, and other gems. Juet and several of the sailors grew wide-eyed at this information. Hudson didn't believe it for a second. If copper was available, he wondered, why did these men have stone knives? If gold, silver, and jewels were there in such abundance, the French would know of it and would already be reaping the wealth. Hudson later wrote in his journal that he suspected the Natives had heard of these things from other white men, and lied about them in hopes of receiving more gifts. After the Natives left, Hudson shattered the dreams of Juet and the others when he told them that the "savages" had never laid eyes on gold, silver, or diamonds.

The following morning dawned clear. The fog was gone at last. The men were anxious to go ashore, but Hudson told them to weigh anchor and take the *Half Moon* a little farther into the bay. They dropped anchor again near the mouth of what is now called the St. George River. Hudson led the initial shore party himself. At about nine o'clock on the morning of July 18, 1609, Henry Hudson set foot on North American soil for the first time. He and his men climbed a hill to get a better look at this wild corner of the New World. Hudson stood in silent awe of what he saw.

Hudson's dream was to find a waterway to the fabulous Orient. But as a man who was at heart an explorer, he could not help but be held breathless when he gazed upon something so astounding, it was beyond the imaginations of even great men like Richard Hakluyt and Peter Plancius. At that time a vast forest, unlike anything that still existed in Western Europe, covered North America from the Atlantic coast to the middle of the continent. A squirrel, leaping from treetop to treetop, could have travelled from the seashore to the eastern bank of the Mississippi River without once touching the ground.

Hudson had never heard of the Mississippi River and he had no idea of the actual size of North America. But he was so moved by the vista of endless forest that he beheld from his hilltop observation point that he made an almost poetic entry in his journal.

> The wilderness of the New World forms a vast natural cathedral. No work of man is its equal. Nowhere is there such natural grandeur. In many places the forest comes down to meet the sea, the green of leaves blending with the green water. I did not know whether to weep or cry aloud with joy, but in my heart of hearts I rejoiced to see the wonders wrought by God.

Since June 15, the *Half Moon* had been plugging along without the benefit of a foremast and the sails it supported. Hudson had spare yardarms in the hold, reluctantly paid for by the directors of the VOC, who at that moment thought he was searching for a Northeast Passage. With the largest forest he had ever seen to choose from, Hudson took a party ashore to cut down a tree, strip it, and fashion it into a mast. While the men worked, Hudson took a walk through the forest, enchanted by what he saw. When the men were finished with their job and went back to the ship, he did not go with them. He wanted to spend some time ashore alone, and he did so with no fear of hostile Natives or any of the dangers of the New World. Later Hudson wrote in his journal,

> Myself remaining on the shore after the dispatch of the men to the ship, I signaled to the quarterdeck from the water's edge soon before sundown, and Juet sent my boat to fetch me and return me safely to the Half Moon.

The next day, July 19, Juet took a party ashore to fill water casks. They found a natural spring with water so pure that the usually caustic Juet wrote, "It has as sweet a taste as brandywine." However, that same day Juet would be back to his usual surly nature, and would find fault with Hudson over a matter almost astonishing in its pettiness.

While the water casks were being filled, two of the men idly wandering along the beach found a lobster in shallow water. They were amazed at how much larger it was than the European lobsters they were familiar with. The other men joined them in a lobster hunt, and they soon had thirty-one to take back to the ship for a feast.

The cook boiled the lobsters, and in a gesture of companionship, Hudson sat down to eat with the men instead of retiring to the privacy of his cabin. He even brought out two jugs of wine from his private stores to share with the men. Hudson wrote of the lobsters, "Their flesh is firm, and their taste more succulent than that of other shell fish." Hudson's observation of the dinner party was positive. "All were merry," he wrote.

But Juet made a much different entry in his journal.

> Cap'n. Hudson ate two lobsters. Colman and I ate one per each as did the men. I saw them looking angrily at the Cap'n., and whilst they dared not speak their grievance, they were wondering why he should have eaten two when they were allowed only one per each.

It was a peculiar attitude for Juet to take, considering the fact that Hudson had shared his wine with the men. Moreover, as there were almost twice as many lobsters as there were men, there was enough for almost everyone to have two. It seemed that Juet would seize upon any excuse to be critical of Hudson.

The men had just finished their meal when the six Natives who had visited previously returned. Hudson had the impression they were looking for more gifts. He asked them about the gold, silver, and jewels they had spoken of on their first visit. They looked at Hudson blankly, as though they did not know what he was talking about.

Then the Natives moved toward the hatches, and the one who spoke some French said that they wished to see the interior of the ship. The sailors, who had been indulging in Hudson's wine, suddenly became alarmed. They thought the Natives planned to steal their belongings. Three sailors jumped up and stood between the Natives and the hatch with drawn knives.

Startled by this sudden show of hostility, the Natives clambered into their canoes and went ashore. Juet wrote of the incident, "The people coming aboard showed us great friendship but we could not trust them."

Early the next morning the man on watch shouted an alarm. Dozens of Natives in canoes were paddling toward the *Half Moon*. Once again Hudson ordered firearms to be distributed to the men. He told the sailors who had been assigned gunnery duty to stand by the cannon. Hudson assumed that the Natives had been offended by the unfriendly reception they'd had a day earlier and now wanted to retaliate.

As the canoes approached, however, the leader who spoke French stood up and said that they had come to trade furs. They were not armed. Hudson agreed to allow the Natives to come aboard a few at a time. The ship's gunners kept a wary eye on the flotilla of canoes.

Hudson did not know much about furs, but he was certain the beaver and fox pelts the Natives brought aboard were of fine quality and would fetch a good price in Amsterdam. He offered the Natives more blankets, beads, and mirrors, but they told him they would only trade for "red gowns." Hudson was puzzled. What did they mean by "red gowns"?

The Native traders called to an elderly man in one of the canoes to come aboard. Hudson almost burst out laughing, but fortunately he managed to keep a straight face. The old man was wearing a red woolen nightshirt that went down to his knees. It was an inexpensive garment that was common in Europe. The old man had obtained his in trade with the French, and now the other men of his community wanted one.

Juet, Colman, and a few of the sailors had red nightshirts which they gladly exchanged for the much more valuable furs.

Hudson handled the bartering, which he did not enjoy. "I felt like a merchant," he wrote contemptuously.

The men spent the next two days cutting trees for spare masts, which they stored in the hold. Hudson sent men out in the ship's boat to fish, and they returned with a large catch of cod and halibut. Another group collected forty lobsters for the cook's pot. The Natives with whom the sailors had traded were camped nearby, and the men saw where they had beached their canoes. Juet noted in his journal, "We kept a good watch for fear of being betrayed by the people."

The Europeans were strangers in a strange land, so it was understandable that they would be on their guard, not entirely trusting the Natives. But so far the local people had shown no hostility whatsoever toward the white visitors. In fact, it was not they who proved themselves capable of treacherous behavior, but the men of the *Half Moon*. If the English and Dutch sailors had been willing to pursue a French ship on the high seas with piracy in mind, they would certainly have no qualms about pillaging a village of "savages."

On July 25, Juet and six men armed with muskets went out in the ship's boat and stole one of the Native canoes, which they took back to the *Half Moon*. This seemed to whet their appetite for plunder. Juet went out again, this time with twelve armed men and two of the ship's small cannon, which Juet called by the slang term "murderers." They advanced on the Native camp. At the sight of the heavily armed strangers, the Natives fled into the woods, leaving behind all of their property. The sailors looted the camp of furs, clothing, and anything else they could carry off. In his journal Juet justified this act of outright larceny. "We ... robbed them, as they would have done to us."

Hudson had to have known what Juet and his party were up to, but he did nothing about it, before or after the fact. Was this because he condoned the raid, or did Hudson once again show that he was a weak commander who could not control his men? One thing was certain: the "savages" would no longer be friendly toward the men of the *Half Moon*. Hudson quite sensibly weighed anchor that night and put his new foremast to the test under full sail. By dawn the *Half Moon* was at sea and miles down the coast, well beyond the reach of the Natives Juet had robbed.

The *Half Moon* slowly made her way southward. Hudson charted the coastline and thought he had sailed into previously undiscovered territory, which he called New Holland, in honour of his employers. Then he realized that he had reached Cape Cod, which had been discovered by the English explorer Captain Bartholomew Gosnold in 1602. Hudson referred to Gosnold in his journal; further evidence that he was as up-to-date on New World explorations as a man of his time could possibly be. Then he went to work improving on Gosnold's geographic information.

Hudson's men went ashore and found wild, sweet grapes. This led to the mistaken belief that the region now known as New England had a Mediterranean climate. No one knew yet of the frigid winters in that part of America. Hudson had peaceful encounters with the local people, and he and Juet both noted that the Native men smoked green tobacco in pipes with copper stems. Copper, of course, would be of interest to the VOC.

The *Half Moon* continued south, and by August 18 was off Virginia, where Captain John Smith had established the Jamestown colony. As he passed the entrance to Chesapeake Bay, Hudson decided against visiting Jamestown. He did not know how a Dutch ship might be received there.

Hudson sailed as far south as what is now Cape Hatteras, North Carolina. He was fortunate he did not encounter any Spanish ships. The Spanish had claimed this territory, and they had no tolerance whatsoever for trespassers.

On August 21, a severe storm lashed the *Half Moon*. A huge wave broke over the bow and struck the foresail so hard that it split the sail. Once again the ship had to lie-a-trie while some men went to work with long needles, mending the sail. Even worse, as far as the highly superstitious sailors were concerned, was the behavior of the ship's cat.

Juet wrote, "Tonight our cat ran crying from one side of the ship to the other, looking overboard. This made us wonder, but we saw nothing." In those days people associated cats with the devil, witchcraft, and evil. Having a cat aboard to keep down the rat population was a practical idea, but sailors always worried that a witch might use the ship's cat as a medium through which to work black magic on the ship and crew. The *Half Moon*'s cat behaving strangely would have been just as unnerving to the crew as an Atlantic gale.

On August 24, Hudson turned north again. Four days later he entered Delaware Bay and became the first European to explore that body of water. He hoped it would be the entrance to a passage to the Pacific Ocean, and was disappointed when shallow water forced him to turn back. This couldn't be the river Captain Smith had told him of. Then on September 2, off present-day Sandy Hook, New Jersey, Hudson found what he was looking for: an outflow of water so great, it had to be coming from a channel that led to the Pacific.

Hudson sailed past the lower tip of a large island whose name would be recorded for the first time in Robert Juet's journal as *Manna-hata*, an Algonquin word meaning "island of many hills." There were actually three main channels to the river mouth. On his initial probes Hudson found the way blocked by shoals. Then he found clear passage between Staten Island and the site of present-day Brooklyn.

Hudson was not the first European to see this river mouth. The Italian explorer Giovanni da Verrazano had been there in 1524, but he had not gone upstream. Hudson would be the first explorer to do that, and so today the river bears his name.

Looking across the broad natural harbour surrounded by forested hills, Hudson could barely contain his excitement. This had to be the river the Natives had told Captain John Smith about. But was it a passage to the Pacific Ocean? There was only one way to find out.

Hudson anchored near Staten Island, and the next morning he sent some men out in the ship's boat to make some preliminary explorations of the waterways and the islands. He had hoped to use the stolen Native canoe for this work, but it had been irreparably damaged in an accident. While they were on their scouting mission the men netted several big fish, including a ray that was so large it took four men to haul it into the boat.

On September 4, Hudson and most of the crew went ashore, setting foot on the mainland of what is now New Jersey. Hudson marvelled at the magnificent trees. "They are of a beauty seldom seen by men," he wrote. Wild plums and grapes grew in abundance. Hudson told one of his men to pick a hatful of grapes to take back to Juet, whom he had left in charge of the *Half Moon*. Perhaps he thought a gift of fresh fruit would sweeten the first mate's sour disposition. One of the Dutch sailors walked through a patch of unfamiliar vegetation and quickly developed burning, itching blisters. The Hudson expedition had discovered poison ivy!

The presence of the *Half Moon* soon attracted the attention of the local people. A large group of men, women, and children arrived in canoes. Juet noted that they wore furs and copper bracelets. Two men who appeared to be leaders wore headdresses of brightly coloured feathers. These people indicated that they wanted to trade tobacco for goods like beads and steel knives. Hudson wrote of the encounter:

> When I came on shore, the swarthy natives all stood around and sung in their fashion; their clothing consisted of the skins of foxes and other animals, which they dress and make the skins into garments of various sorts. Their food is Turkish wheat [maize or Indian corn], whey they cook by baking, and is excellent eating. They all came ... in their canoes, which are made of a single hollowed tree; their weapons are bows and arrows, pointed with sharp stones, which they fasten with hard resin. They had no houses, but slept under the blue heavens, sometimes on mats of bulrushes interwoven, and sometimes on the leaves of trees. They always carry with them all their goods, such as their food and green tobacco, which is strong and good for use. They appear to be a friendly people, but have a great propensity to steal, and are exceedingly adroit in carrying away whatever they take a fancy to.

The Natives told Hudson through sign language that he was at the mouth of a long and mighty river. This was the kind of information Hudson wanted to hear. On the morning of September 6, he sent second mate John Colman and four other men out in the ship's boat to do some further reconnoitering.

The men rowed through a gap now called the Narrows and then raised the gig's sail. They landed on Manhattan Island at a place about fourteen miles from where the *Half Moon* lay at anchor. Wild flowers were in bloom, carpeting the ground with an array of bright colours and filling the air with a sweet fragrance. It was as though the men had found paradise. They came upon some wild celery, which they thought was delicious. Then, suddenly and completely unexpectedly, tragedy struck.

As Colman's party was returning to their ship, a heavy fog rolled in. Then two canoes glided out of the mist, coming straight for them. One held fourteen men and the other held twelve. Without provocation, the warriors fired a volley of arrows. Colman was killed when an arrow pierced his throat. Two other sailors were wounded. Then, as inexplicably as they had made the assault, the warriors broke off the attack and disappeared back into the fog.

The surviving sailors could not find their way back to the *Half Moon* in the darkness and fog. They tossed out their anchor, but the current was too strong for it to hold the gig stationary. The men rowed back and forth all night, fearful that the Natives would come again to finish them off. In the morning the fog burned away, and at 10:00 a.m. the men returned to the *Half Moon* with Colman's body.

Hudson was stunned. He had not lost a single man on either of his previous voyages. Now here was his second mate, murdered for no good reason by treacherous "savages"! Could the attackers have been the very people who had been trading with them? The ship's company took the body to the mainland and buried it at a place they called Colman's Point, believed to be near Sandy Hook. The burial ceremony was brief, because the men felt vulnerable to attack on land.

When they returned to the ship, Hudson had the gig taken aboard. Then he had boarding put all around the rails as a defensive measure. He ordered the cannon to be loaded and primed for immediate action. The men were told to keep weapons close at hand, but were under strict orders not to shoot unless the captain or the first mate gave the command. For the rest of the day and throughout the night, sentries patrolled the deck and a lookout kept watch in the crow's nest.

The next morning, just after dawn, the lookout shouted that several Natives were approaching in a canoe. As the canoe drew near, Hudson could see that it contained several large, bulky sacks made of woven reeds. The Natives did not appear to be armed.

Looking down from the rail, Juet indicated that he wanted to see what was in the sacks. The Natives opened them, and he could see that they were full of the grain that Europeans called Indian corn. The Natives had come to trade, and gave no sign that they knew anything about the attack.

Hudson allowed the Natives to climb aboard one at a time, and each man was searched for weapons. Hudson was satisfied that they were not armed, but he was still suspicious. He took them to the poop deck, where the gig lay covered by a tarpaulin. The four survivors of Colman's party, two of them with their bandaged wounds, were also there. At Hudson's command the tarpaulin was pulled away, revealing the gig. It was still spattered with Colman's blood.

Hudson closely watched the faces and eyes of the Natives. He was looking for any sign that these men knew about the attack. But the sight of the bloodstained boat and the wounded sailors brought no response at all from the Natives. Hudson still didn't know for certain if they were innocent, or if they were very good actors. He decided that for the time being he would give them the benefit of a doubt. The Natives accepted some beads and mirrors for the corn, and then left. Hudson wrote in his journal, "Had they indicated by a cunning light in their eyes that they had knowledge of the foul murder, I was prepared to order my company to exterminate all without delay."

The men on the *Half Moon* spent another day and night in what was virtually a state of siege. They did not know who in the surrounding wilderness was friend or foe. Like most of their European contemporaries, they looked upon all of the Native peoples of the New World as barbarians.

The next morning, September 9, two canoes that Hudson called "great longboats" came speeding across the water toward the *Half Moon*. Each boat carried about twenty warriors armed with bows and arrows, and spears. As the Natives drew near, they indicated that they wanted to trade.

Hudson didn't trust them. He waited until they were close to the ship and then fired a warning shot from a pistol. At the loud report of the gun, the men in one canoe made a hasty retreat for the shore. Hudson pulled a second pistol from his belt and pointed it at the other canoe, which was closer to the ship. The Natives were clearly frightened at the sight of the gun. Their fear verged on panic when sailors lined the rail of the ship and aimed muskets at them. Through signs, Juet told them that he wanted two warriors to come aboard the ship as hostages. The Natives had no choice but to comply. Hudson believed that having hostages aboard would provide security against attack.

With his men now armed at all times, and ever on the alert, Hudson took a few days to finish mapping the vast harbour and its islands. On September 12, he sailed six miles up the river before dropping anchor. A flotilla of canoes full of men, women, and children came out to the ship. The people appeared peaceful, but Hudson would not allow any of them aboard. The Natives traded some beans and oysters for a few trinkets and then departed.

For the next few days the *Half Moon* sailed up the broad river, anchoring at night. On September 15, the two Native captives somehow got out of the hold where they'd been confined, jumped overboard, and swam ashore. Once they were on land they laughed and shouted in scorn at the men on the ship. Hudson considered sending a party of men after them, but then thought better of it. The Europeans did not know the woods the way the Natives did, and could easily find themselves in a very dangerous situation.

As the ship moved upstream, Hudson marvelled at the pristine beauty of the river valley, at the abundance of wildlife, and the numerous schools of salmon and other fish. He was especially impressed with the high bluffs that are now called the Palisades. He wrote in his journal:

> Nature was in one of her happier moods when she created these cliffs. They stretch for approximately fifteen miles on the west bank of the river, and are ever a delight to the eye. Behind this natural wall stretches the great forest, which lies like a cloak over most of the New World. The river flows swiftly, and many birds circle and soar overhead. I have recognized the osprey and the heron, larger than their like in England, and others whose names I do not know. These latter may be birds known only to the continent wherein we now journey … I doubt not that there is much game to be found

in the forest. On cliff ledges I have seen the nests of birds, and would like the taste of fresh eggs on my palate. But, it having been proved to our sorrow that the natives hereabouts are blood-thirsty, I dare not send a landing party ashore for fear that more of my men will be foully and wantonly murdered.

Hudson's suspicions about the Natives diminished somewhat as he sailed farther upstream. The people who lived along the river came out in their canoes to look at the strange vessel. They seemed genuinely friendly, and Hudson could detect nothing in their behavior that suggested there might be ulterior motives behind the smiles. Finally, on September 18, he felt enough at ease to accept an invitation to have supper with an elderly chief. Juet, who accompanied Hudson, described the chief as "a governor of this country."

While he was in the Native village, Hudson took careful mental notes of everything he saw. Later he wrote detailed descriptions of the people's homes, food, and lifestyle. He explained that the women and boys laboured over crops, while the men hunted and fished. Hudson provided a vivid account of his visit to the chief's home.

On our coming into the house, two mats were spread out to sit upon. Immediately some food was spread, served in well-made wooden bowls. This food was a paste, grey-brown in colour, with a distinctive odour that I could not recognize. I was loathe to eat it, but the old man ate from his bowl, dipping in his fingers and letting the substance cling to them. So great was his hospitality and so jovial his manner that I was sensible to his feelings and did eat, too. The food had a taste both familiar and strange, and when I made enquiry, the old man showed me it was a pulp taken from the inner rind of trees, which was mashed and mixed with whortleberries.

Two men were dispatched at once in quest of game, who soon after brought in a pair of pigeons they had shot with bows and arrows. The skill of the Indians with these weapons is very great … They likewise killed a fat dog, and skinned it in great haste with shells they had got out of the water. Then they roasted it, and when it was cooked they cut pieces of meat with shell knives and ate it with their fingers. In my own land dogs are members of a man's household and are not eaten. But I was again sensible to the feelings of my host, and cut myself a portion with my knife, Juet doing likewise. The taste was not sickening, as I feared, and had I not seen the dog killed, would have thought I was eating freshly roasted pork.

The Indians supposed that I would remain with them for the night. But I could not abandon my men to the elements, nor my ship to the mercies of savages who might be otherwise than good-humoured, and after the dinner was done made ready to return to my ship.

The natives are a very good people, for when they saw I would not remain, they supposed that

I was afraid of their bows, and taking their arrows, they broke them in pieces and threw them into the fire … I gave them a gift of knives before I took my leave of them, although Juet was fearful that these weapons might be turned against us. But I had already judged the character of the old man and his people, and know we had nought to fear from them. Their gratitude at receiving such knives, on which we ourselves place so little value, gave me the greatest satisfaction I have known since I began my voyage up the river.

Hudson went on to describe the lushness of the forest and the incredible fertility of the soil. He clearly stated, "Were our own industrious farmers to settle here, they would soon transform this wilderness into a Paradise where no man need ever go hungry … Never have I beheld such a rich and pleasant land." While other explorers of the time sought only the glitter of gold and silver, Hudson envisioned a thriving agricultural colony.

Yet, even as he gushed over the beauty of the river valley and the possibilities for settlement, Hudson felt pangs of disappointment. He was beginning to think that perhaps this was not a passage to the Pacific after all. By September 19, the *Half Moon* had reached the site of present-day Albany. Hudson found that beyond this point, the channel was too narrow and shallow to accommodate a ship. Moreover, the old chief had told him there was no salt sea at the headwaters of the river.

Nonetheless, Hudson would not be satisfied until his own men investigated. He had the ship's carpenter fit the gig with a taller mast, enabling it to carry a larger sail and thus sail upstream against the current. Then he sent his bo'sun upriver with four other men. The scouting party went about six miles before turning back with the crushing news that the river above the *Half Moon*'s present anchorage was not navigable.

On the morning of September 21, Hudson was about to weigh anchor to begin his journey downriver, when a group of Natives appeared. These were Mohawks from the town of Schenectadea, near the confluence of the Hudson and Mohawk rivers. Something about these people made Hudson and his men uneasy. Hudson invited the chief and two warriors into his cabin, where he and Juet gave them large quantities of brandywine. Hudson's intent was to "try whether they had any treachery in them."

The Natives had never before experienced alcohol, and so they were soon drunk. They laughed, sang, and cavorted around the cabin. One of the men had brought his wife along, and Juet noted that she "sat as modestly as any of our women would have done in a strange place."

Finally, the chief passed out. The others, intoxicated and bewildered, were afraid that the white men had put a spell on them. They left the ship, taking their comatose leader with them.

The following morning the Mohawks returned and gave Hudson an unusual gift: several leather belts that had shells sewn into them. Hudson eventually learned that this was "wampum," a form of currency in which the Natives placed great value. Evidently the chief had still not awakened from his drinking binge, and his people might have been trying to pay Hudson to lift the "spell." Later the chief woke up, feeling none the worse for wear. His relieved people brought Hudson more wampum, some tobacco, and a side of venison.

Hudson began his trip downstream on September 23. Due to strong winds the *Half Moon* ran aground twice. Once, while the ship was at anchor, the chief who had overindulged in brandywine caught up with her, accompanied by several warriors and members of his family. He had brought food and tobacco, for which Hudson exchanged knives and blankets. Hudson did not offer his guests any more liquor, and in his journal he advised against giving alcohol to the Natives. "The Red Indians of the New World cannot drink spirits with equanimity … these primitive people become crazed after they drink only a small amount."

On his way downstream Hudson paid a brief visit to the old chief with whom he'd shared supper, but did not tarry long. The days were becoming cooler, and he realized that the season was getting on. He traded for food and furs with several groups of Natives who came out to the ship, but he was now more interested in putting the New World behind him before winter set in.

Then, on October 1, another band of Natives boarded the ship to trade pelts. While business was being carried out on deck, one man in a canoe got behind the vessel and climbed onto the rudder. Thinking himself unobserved, he climbed through a porthole into Juet's cabin and stole a pillow, two shirts, and two bandoliers. As he climbed out again, he was seen. The bo'sun killed him with a blast from a blunderbuss.

Now there was pandemonium on the *Half Moon*. A blunderbuss was a type of shotgun, and when discharged it sounded like a clap of thunder. The terrified Natives couldn't get off the ship fast enough. A few scrambled into their canoes, but others jumped over the side into the river and swam for shore. Two got into the canoe with the dead man and Juet's property.

The gig was in the water, so Juet and several other men, including the cook, piled into it and began a pursuit. They overtook a Native who was swimming. The man reached up and grabbed the gig by the gunwhale, evidently thinking he could capsize it. The cook chopped the Native's hand off with a sword, and the man sank into the river.

On shore Juet's party found the abandoned canoe with his belongings still in it. They recovered the property and quickly returned to the ship. Hudson weighed anchor and put on as much sail as he dared. He wanted to get as far from that place as he could before nightfall.

Before the crew could weigh anchor the next morning, they saw more canoes full of warriors coming toward the ship. The Natives indicated that they wanted to come aboard. But as they drew near, Hudson recognized one of the men who had recently been a hostage. He warned them to stay away.

While half the crew winched up the anchor and unfurled sails, Juet and the rest stood ready with weapons. Two canoes suddenly swept behind the ship and the warriors loosed a volley of arrows. The arrows pierced sails and thudded into timbers, but did not hit any sailors. In reply Juet's men fired their muskets, killing two or three Natives.

Once again awed by the noise and killing power of the white men's weapons, the Natives quickly withdrew. The *Half Moon* fled downstream, carried swiftly by the current and a favouring wind. But the Natives were not as intimidated by the gunfire as Hudson had hoped.

A short distance ahead of the ship, a point of land jutted out into the river. There, over a hundred warriors waited for the *Half Moon* to come within range of their bows. A ship under sail is not as easily manoeuvred as a canoe. Hudson could see that he would not be able to swing the vessel far enough out into the river to avoid a rain of deadly arrows. He immediately told Juet to fire on the Natives with a small cannon called a "falcon." Juet wrote of the incident, "There I shot a Falcon at them and killed two of them whereupon the rest fled into the woods."

Even as the main body of the Native force withdrew, about ten bravely pressed the attack. They leapt into a war canoe and attempted to intercept the *Half Moon*. Juet fired the falcon again. The cannonball smashed into the canoe, killing one warrior. A volley of musket fire killed three or four more of the men who were now struggling in the water. Hudson didn't wait to see if the others made it to shore or drowned. He continued downriver with all speed, not even anchoring for the night. The *Half Moon* did not stop until she was once again off the island of Manhattan.

On October 2, the *Half Moon* was anchored off the site of present-day Hoboken. A heavy fog had rolled in, reducing visibility to almost zero. Unable to set sail, and still fearful of attack, Hudson kept armed sailors on watch. But, as Juet recorded, "No people came to trouble us and we rode quietly all night, although with much wind and rain."

The next day a squall swept in, and the tide and current were so strong the *Half Moon* drifted, dragging her anchor. Not until October 4 did the weather clear, allowing Hudson to at last make for the open sea. The river the English captain had explored and charted was not a short route to the Pacific, but it held great promise for colonization.

With his river adventures behind him, Hudson faced a dilemma. He wanted to sail north and investigate the Furious Overfall, but it was much too late in the season for that. And to what extent could he trust this crew? Hudson discussed the situation with his officers.

The bo'sun favoured wintering in Newfoundland and then sailing for the Furious Overfall in the spring. Robert Juet was sullen and evasive. Evidently he would not venture an opinion until he knew what the rest of the crew wanted to do.

Hudson knew that the prospect of a winter in Newfoundland would not sit well with the Dutch sailors. Winters there were harsh, and the fishing ports were abandoned during the cold months. Nonetheless, Hudson suggested to the bo'sun that he casually sound the men out on the idea.

The information the bo'sun brought back to Hudson was mixed. None of the Dutch sailors wanted to go to the Furious Overfall, but they were apprehensive about returning to Amsterdam. They were afraid that Hudson might yet report them as mutineers, especially now that Captain John Smith's river had proven to be a dead end. A few of the former sea beggars even suggested that they take the *Half Moon* south to the Spanish Main and turn pirate.

The English sailors wanted to go home. The supply of salted and pickled beef was gone, and they were tired of eating fish. On an extended voyage, they would have nothing to look forward to but short rations of cod and herring. Hudson wrote later,

> In my heart I could not blame them. No man is courageous on an empty stomach. The last of our ale was long since drunk, and there were no spirits on board except the last cask of brandy-wine from my own store.

Hudson had all the crew assemble on deck and offered a compromise. They would go to Ireland, where they could obtain meat, ale, and other supplies. Then in the spring they would sail to the Furious Overfall for another chance at the Northwest Passage and the glory and fortune that would come with its discovery.

Ireland had the advantage of being closer to the Furious Overfall than Amsterdam.

The men unanimously agreed to this idea. But somewhere in the mid-Atlantic something happened on the *Half Moon*. Neither Hudson nor Juet said anything about it in their journals. Possibly some of the men changed their minds and threatened mutiny if Hudson didn't give up the idea of taking them to the Furious Overfall. In a letter he wrote later to the Dutch East Indian Company, Hudson complained about seven Dutch sailors whom he said were "lacking in efficiency," which may have been a diplomatic way of saying they were insubordinate. Whatever the reason, the *Half Moon* did not sail into an Irish port. Instead, on November 7, she dropped anchor in the harbour of Dartmouth, in Devonshire, England. Hudson was home … and would soon be in trouble!

7

Arrest and Reprieve

As summer gave way to autumn in 1609, the directors of the VOC had become deeply concerned when the *Half Moon* did not return to Amsterdam. They feared that the ship had been crushed in the icy seas north of Russia. The financial cost of such a disaster was more than the Dutch businessmen cared to contemplate. All the money the incorrigible Hudson had compelled them to invest in the voyage — gone! Their ship, the *Half Moon* — gone! The dream of a profitable short route to China — gone! To make the financial situation even more unpleasant, they would have to pay a death benefit to Hudson's widow, in accordance with their contract. They would have been very surprised indeed if they had been aware on that November 7, that their ship was in the English port of Dartmouth.

At that time, Dartmouth was a rough, almost lawless port. It was the main base for the English cod fishery, but it was also a haven for pirates and smugglers. Legitimate ship captains often avoided Dartmouth, because their crewmen would be tempted to jump ship and go for the easy money in piracy and smuggling. London merchants, like the men of the Muscovy Company, hated Dartmouth because it was beyond their control. That may have been why Hudson went there.

Thomas Holland, the mayor of Dartmouth, was surprised to see a Dutch ship in the harbour. He arranged to meet the ship's master, and was even more surprised to learn that the captain was an Englishman. Hudson was about to find himself once again a major player in a potentially deadly game of intrigue.

In addition to being a provincial official, Thomas Holland was a spy for Sir Robert Cecil, the Earl of Salisbury. Cecil was Lord High Treasurer of England and Secretary of State to King James I. It was essential for a man who held two very high posts to know everything that was going on in the country. He would certainly want to know why a foreign ship under an English captain unexpectedly showed up in an English harbour. Holland set about questioning Hudson, without letting the captain know that he was, in fact, being interrogated. Hudson responded to the questions perhaps a little too cooperatively, making sure to mention the names of some of the Englishmen he knew who were in high places. It was as though Hudson desired to slyly pass on to certain Englishmen information that was supposed to be for VOC ears only, and at the same time let the people in England who sponsored voyages of discovery know that he was available. Hudson was keeping his options open. Just in case the Dutch didn't hire him again, he wanted to cultivate possibilities in England. But it was a game that could prove dangerous.

Hudson told Holland all about the unusual voyage of the *Half Moon*. He said that several of his men were sick with scurvy, so he had put in at Dartmouth to give them a chance to recuperate. In the spring, Hudson said, he intended to sail back to the New World. Holland was impressed with Hudson, calling him "a man of experience" in the long letter he wrote to Sir Robert Cecil. But Holland also suspected that Hudson was withholding information: "it seems to me, by conferring with him, that he has discovered some especial matters of great consequence which he would not impart."

Hudson, meanwhile, had written to the VOC, telling them about the wonderful river valley he had explored. He brazenly asked for the incredible sum of fifteen hundred florins to outfit for a new expedition to the Furious Overfall. He said he would leave Dartmouth in March, stop at Newfoundland to fill the *Half Moon*'s hold with salted fish, and then sail on to explore the Furious Overfall. He would return in the fall, stopping to sell the salted cod in Scotland, where it brought the best price. Hudson was so preoccupied with planning his next voyage, two weeks passed before he wrote to tell Katherine that he was in England.

Hudson's letter was quite possibly carried by the VOC agent who had sailed with him. The ship on which the messenger travelled was delayed by a storm, so the letter did not reach Amsterdam until the end of December. After reading Hudson's account of his adventures, the enraged merchants responded with a letter of their own, demanding that Hudson return to Amsterdam with their ship immediately. They now believed that Hudson had duped them into letting him use their money and ship to carry out explorations for the ultimate benefit of England. They weren't entirely wrong. Hudson allowed English cartographers to make copies of the charts and maps he had made for the Dutch.

While Hudson's letter was making its slow journey to Amsterdam, news of Hudson's work for the Dutch reached King

James, quite likely through Sir Robert Cecil. It was not unusual for an English sea captain to work for a foreign company, but it appeared to James and his advisors that Hudson had done some remarkably good work for the Dutch East India Company, whether his employers appreciated it or not.

The English had more or less given up on the idea of a practical Northeast Passage, so they had not been concerned when Hudson ventured out to search for it for the Dutch. But now they had an admission from Hudson himself that he had taken his search west, where there was a very strong possibility that a passage to the Pacific existed. Sailing for Dutch employers in a Dutch ship, Hudson had trespassed in the coastal waters of Virginia, giving Dutch sailors knowledge of the seas off an English colony. The Dutch could one day put that knowledge to their own advantage.

Sailing under a Dutch flag, Hudson had explored a new and very promising river valley, thus giving the Dutch a strong legal claim to that territory. Now Hudson was in an English port, awaiting instructions from Amsterdam, with the intention of sailing off again to explore the Furious Overfall and find a Northwest Passage ... for the Dutch! The more the king discussed the matter with his advisors, the angrier he became. There were those among his most influential counsellors who suggested that Captain Henry Hudson was guilty of treason!

In Dartmouth, Hudson was living in his quarters aboard the *Half Moon* and completing his charts and journal. In accordance with his contract, he sent these vitally important documents to Amsterdam. However, the journal Hudson sent to the directors of the VOC was a copy that contained only the information he wanted them to see. He kept the original. The abridged version that arrived at East India House was filed away and preserved for posterity. Hudson's personal copy would disappear forever.

In mid-December, Hudson prepared to go to London to spend Christmas with his family. His English sailors had nothing to keep them in Dartmouth, so they decided to travel with the captain. Most of the Dutch sailors went home, expecting to return in several weeks. A few men were left to watch over the *Half Moon*. Hudson didn't know that he would never set foot on the *Half Moon* again. Months would pass before English authorities would finally allow the ship to return to Amsterdam.

Hudson, his son John, Juet, and a few English sailors started for London on rented horses. The captain was in a good mood. He was cheerfully talkative, evidently determined to enjoy the ride through the countryside along England's notoriously bad roads. Juet enjoyed neither the English countryside nor Hudson's jovial company. He wrote in his journal, "He entertained us on the road with stories, but his humour left much to be desired."

The sour-minded Juet soon had a much greater cause for concern than Hudson's stories. A few hours after Hudson's party left Dartmouth, they were stopped on the road by a squad of armed soldiers. These men were from the king's personal regiment. The commanding officer gave Hudson a document that bore the official seal of the Privy Council, the highest legislative body in England. When Hudson broke the seal and opened the parchment, he saw that he had been served with an Order-in-Council. It severely reprimanded Henry Hudson, captain and master, for working for a foreign power, "to the detriment of his own country." It stated that Hudson and all English members of his crew were forbidden to leave England without first obtaining royal approval.

The Order-in-Council did not flatly accuse Hudson of being a traitor. However, he could read between the lines, and he knew that the inference was there. That, and the gruff manner of the soldiers, indicated to Hudson that he could very well be imprisoned in the Tower of London, and then hauled into court to face charges of treason. An angry Juet, writing of the incident later said, "We were treated like murderers or other criminals of the most despicable sort. From the moment we encountered the King's men, we were held under close arrest."

Hudson had good reason to fear for his life. Men with far more powerful connections than he had been charged with treason after incurring the wrath of a monarch, and had lost their heads for it. At that very moment Sir Walter Raleigh, a soldier, writer, and explorer who was once a favourite of Queen Elizabeth I, was imprisoned in the Tower, waiting for King James to decide whether or not he should be executed.

Hudson was kept under surveillance. Soldiers were posted outside his home, and if he left the house they accompanied him wherever he went. It embarrassed and depressed Hudson to have soldiers following him everywhere, so he stayed home. He did not even go to church with his family on Christmas morning. At any moment the soldiers could receive orders to take him to prison. Hudson hoped that his fame as an explorer would entitle him to an apartment in the Tower, where he would at least be imprisoned in comfort. The alternative was a filthy, rat-infested dungeon in a common jail.

In January, while he was still awaiting the king's pleasure, Hudson received the letter from the VOC, demanding that he return to Amsterdam with their ship. Rather than write a letter in reply, Hudson copied the text of the Order-in-Council in his own hand, and sent it to Amsterdam. Surprisingly, the VOC directors became angry at what they considered mistreatment of Hudson. At their request, the Dutch government instructed its ambassador in London, Emanuel Van Meteran, to go to Whitehall and personally lodge a protest on Hudson's behalf.

Van Meteran had an audience with James during which he not only defended Hudson, but also suggested that the English government's actions against the captain were endangering the good relations between their countries. The king replied that he valued his friendship with the Dutch, and he congratulated them on the fine river valley Hudson had discovered for them. But he refused to revoke the Order-in-Council.

The story of Hudson's disgrace in the eyes of the king spread across London, and then England. There was a great deal of sympathy for the captain, who was seen as a national hero. Commoners said that Hudson was being punished for no good reason. Aristocrats who had never been happy with the idea of James, a Scot, on the throne of England, championed Hudson's cause.

One man who was particularly interested in Hudson's case was Sir Thomas Smythe, a highly successful and very prominent merchant. Smythe was a founding member of the English East India Company, and formerly the English ambassador to Russia. He firmly believed that exploration and discovery were essential to the expansion of trade, which the English needed if they were to keep pace with the Dutch. He even used his own house as a school for sea captains. Sailors went there in search of work. Henry Hudson had no doubt been a frequent visitor.

Sir Thomas discussed Hudson's situation with two friends. One was Sir Dudley Digges, an admirer of Hudson. His family was wealthy, powerful, and had a background in navigation. The other was John Wolstenholme, a prominent landowner who was the collector of customs for the Port of London, and who had a great interest in exploration.

These three men believed that a Northwest Passage existed. Moreover, they had unshakable faith that Henry Hudson was

Sir Dudley Digges.

the man who could find it. They also felt that if Hudson had discovered a magnificent river valley for the Dutch, he could make an equally spectacular discovery for the English. Had the captain not already given England the rich Spitzbergen whaling grounds? Something the peevish king seemed to have forgotten!

Smythe, Digges, and Wolstenholme went to see Hudson. The guards at Hudson's door made no attempt to interfere with them. These were three very influential men, and everyone knew that Sir Thomas Smythe was a friend of both the king and his heir, Henry the Prince of Wales.

The visitors found Hudson in a depressed mood. He believed he was permanently disgraced. He thought he would be fortunate to escape imprisonment — or worse — and he had no hope that he would ever command a ship again.

Sir Thomas had one question for Hudson: would he be interested in leading an expedition to find the Northwest Passage, on an English ship, and fully financed by English money? Hudson could not believe his ears. Wolstonholme wrote to his wife, "Captain Hudson's pleasure was so great that he leapt out of his chair with joy, sending it crashing to the floor."

Sir Thomas and his colleagues had what they wanted from Hudson: his commitment to search for the Northwest Passage. They hadn't doubted for a moment that they would get it. But there was still the problem of the king and the Order-in-Council. The Order did not forbid Hudson to work for an English employer, but it did prevent him from leaving England without royal permission.

Sir Thomas knew better that to attempt to argue Hudson's case with James, who had a reputation for being unforgiving toward anyone he felt had offended him or threatened the security of his realm. Instead, he, Digges, and Wolstenholme requested an audience with the Prince of Wales.

Sixteen-year-old Prince Henry (who would die at the age of eighteen), was an avid student of the arts, science, and geography. He also had the courage to stand up to his father. The prince had even spoken in support of Sir Walter Raleigh. Prince

Henry agreed to a private interview with Hudson. The next day, Hudson and his three friends went to the meeting at an office the prince kept at 17 Fleet Street in London. The king's soldiers trotted along behind them, still keeping an eye on the alleged traitor.

Hudson knew that his future as a professional navigator, and perhaps his very life, were at stake. He quickly realized that Prince Henry was well informed in matters of navigation, geography, and exploration. His questions were direct and intelligent. Hudson respectfully and sensibly answered in kind. The prince was impressed with Hudson. He promised that he would speak to his father.

Two days later, Prince Henry happily announced that the surveillance of Hudson would end immediately. The captain would be receiving a new commission to find the Northwest Passage for the greater glory of England. King James had, in fact, been glad to be presented with a way in which he could restore Hudson to favour without losing face himself.

Smythe, Digges, and Wolstenholme formed a new enterprise which they called the Company of Gentlemen, with themselves as chief directors. Fifteen other noblemen and merchants, some of them members of the Muscovy Company, were the principle investors. The British East India Company invested three hundred pounds. The Prince of Wales gave the venture royal blessing by making a token investment. To give the new company full credibility, Prince Henry and King James met Hudson publicly at Whitehall, in mid-April.

Many of those who invested money in the expedition had high hopes that in addition to discovering the Northwest Passage, Hudson would find riches in the New World. During the exploration of the river, Robert Juet had written in his journal that he had seen cliff faces that he was certain contained gold and silver. He and some fellow sailors had talked about it in the taverns and other public places. Time would show that there was no gold or silver in the Hudson River Valley, but in that spring of 1610, Englishmen with money were willing to gamble on Henry Hudson as the man who could increase their fortunes.

Hudson himself was working without pay. Sir Thomas Smythe had gone out of his way to help Hudson, but the nobleman was also a businessman. He felt that Hudson had been well rewarded simply by being restored to royal favour. Hudson agreed. He was out of the king's doghouse, and he was finally getting what he'd been dreaming about for years: a ship and a chance at the Furious Overfall. He expected there would be financial rewards enough after he found the Northwest Passage. Hudson had never been in it for the money. He craved glory.

Hudson hadn't been entirely happy with his previous ships, the *Hopewell* and the *Half Moon*. He was overjoyed when Sir Thomas told him that the Company of Gentlemen had purchased a famous ship. The *Discovery* was the vessel in which Captain George Weymouth had first probed the Furious Overfall in 1602. To Hudson, walking the quarterdeck of that ship would be an honour.

The exact dimensions of the bark *Discovery* are not known, but she was larger than the *Hopewell* and the *Half Moon*; broader in the beam and longer. She probably weighed about seventy tons. The *Discovery* handled well in heavy seas, and had a stout hull especially constructed for sailing amidst the ice packs of the northern ocean.

Hudson had a free hand in hiring the crew. With the Company of Gentlemen paying top wages, and Prince Henry's royal sponsorship bringing great prestige, Hudson could choose from the very best mariners in England. Some of the choices he made indicate that Hudson was not a very good judge of character.

Once again Hudson inexplicably hired Robert Juet as first mate. Three other men Hudson chose had sailed with him before: ship's carpenter Philip Staffe, and seamen Arnold Lodlowe, and Michael Perce. Presumably, all had shown themselves to be reliable crewmen.

The quartermaster was a man named John King. He came with good recommendations, but was known to be ill-tempered. The bo'sun was Francis Clements, who at the age of forty was a veteran sailor. Second mate was Robert Bylot, a superb mariner, but a man whose trustworthiness was questionable. The other crewmembers were Sylvanus Bond (cooper), Bennett Matthew (cook), Nicholas Simms (ship's boy), John Williams (gunner), Michael Butt, Adam Moore, Syracke Fanning, William Wilson, John Thomas, and Adrian Motter. John Hudson was also registered as a ship's boy.

For the first time Hudson would have a ship's doctor aboard. Edward Wilson (no relation to seaman William Wilson) was a twenty-two-year-old physician from Portsmouth. He had never been to sea before, and looked forward to the voyage as an adventure.

Another young man going to sea for the first time was Thomas Woodhouse. He was an undergraduate mathematics student at Oxford, and a friend of Sir Dudley Digges. Woodhouse was sailing with Hudson on the recommendation of Sir Dudley, who wanted the youth to get some practical training, so Hudson was obliged to welcome him aboard.

Listed as a "passenger" on the *Discovery* was Abacuck Prickett, a former haberdasher who was now a valet to Sir Dudley Digges. He was quite likely on board to act as the eyes and ears of the

Company of Gentlemen. He was literate, and so could keep his own journal, thus providing the directors with an account of the voyage to go along with the captain's. Prickett always put on a pleasant face when dealing with his superiors, but he was, in fact, a schemer.

Even though Hudson wanted Juet as first mate, the Company of Gentlemen insisted on giving him a man named William Coleburne as "master's mate." Coleburne had been first mate to George Weymouth in 1602. Weymouth had said that he was "a skillful man in his profession." Coleburne, like Prickett, might have been put aboard as a company agent. Sir Thomas Smythe and his partners had a lot of faith in Hudson, but they were also aware of his tendency to veer away from courses set for him by his employers. An officer like Coleburne, carrying a certain degree of authority from the directors, could ensure that Hudson did not go astray.

One other man was destined to sail on the *Discovery*, though not as an official member of the crew. Henry Greene was a young man from a respectable family in Kent, but he had a very bad reputation. He was foul mouthed, irreligious, and sharp tongued. He was a spendthrift who enjoyed the company of London's riff-raff; prostitutes, gamblers, and thieves. Prickett wrote of Greene, "By his lewd life and conversation he lost the good will of all his friends, and had spent all that he had."

Greene showed up at Hudson's door one day with several letters of introduction, including one from his mother. Mrs. Greene apparently hoped that if the famous captain would take the young wastrel under his wing, perhaps he would change his foolish ways. Hudson was still in disgrace with the king when Henry Greene came calling, so perhaps it soothed his battered ego to have a young admirer around. That could explain why Hudson took a liking to Greene.

Hudson took Greene into his house. When Hudson was given command of a new expedition, he told Greene he would take him along, and pay him out of his own pocket. Hudson promised that when they returned to England, he would use his influence to secure Greene a place in Prince Henry's personal guard.

Hudson wrote to Greene's mother, telling her that Henry needed five pounds to fit himself out for sea. Mrs. Greene did not send the money to her son, who could not be trusted with it. Instead she sent the five pounds to a family friend who purchased the necessary items.

Meanwhile, Katherine Hudson developed a great dislike for the young libertine her husband had brought into their home. She objected to Greene's unsavoury friends, who treated the Hudson residence as though it were a tavern. Katherine complained to Hudson, but to no avail.

Hudson's relationship with Henry Greene was as mysterious as his relationship with Robert Juet. Even though Juet said in his journal that Greene had, "the broad shoulders of a river bargeman and even greater strength," he was not a sailor. So why would Hudson want him aboard the *Discovery*? One possible explanation is that Hudson wanted a chronicler for this most important expedition.

Greene was apparently much better educated than Hudson. He had the literary skills to write a vivid and dramatic account of the magnificent voyage upon which Hudson was about to embark. Such a book, once it was published in England, would not only guarantee Hudson further prestigious commands, it would also elevate his name to the ranks of England's most acclaimed maritime heroes. He would be as honoured as the great Sir Francis Drake!

Hudson kept his plan to take Greene along secret. Smythe, Digges, and Wolstenholme would undoubtedly have strong reservations about so notorious a character being aboard their ship on such an important expedition. Greene's name did not appear on the ship's manifest.

In the weeks leading up to the departure date, the *Discovery* was brought up to full readiness for Arctic sailing. Prince Henry had the work done by the very best craftsmen. Sir Thomas Smythe wanted Hudson to have whatever he needed. Therefore, the *Discovery* was equipped with both a small ship's boat and a larger shallop.

The *Discovery* was stocked with enough food to last eight months. That was not enough for a journey all the way to the Orient. Hudson's orders were to explore the Furious Overfall to determine if it was indeed the key to the Northwest Passage. He might even have been instructed to find a suitable harbour where a base could be established. Hudson's employers expected him to be back in England by the end of the year. Hudson had other ideas.

8

Beyond the Furious Overfall

On April 17 — a month later than Hudson would have liked to have departed — all was ready. Early that morning, Hudson attended church services with his family and his men. Katherine was accustomed to seeing her husband go off on long voyages, but she could not hold back the tears when John gave her a farewell embrace.

Aboard the *Discovery*, which was anchored in St. Katherine's Pool, Hudson gave Prince Henry a tour of the ship. He drank a toast with the prince and Sir Thomas Smythe to a successful voyage. Hudson went ashore with them while the crew prepared to sail. Richard Hakluyt was waiting on the dock to say goodbye. Oddly, Hakluyt was not optimistic about this voyage. He told Hudson not to place too much hope in the Furious Overfall being the gateway to the Northwest Passage. "It would be a boon to all mankind it there were such a passage," he said. "But nature is seldom that kind."

Hudson had no time to argue with his friend. Juet was calling impatiently from the quarterdeck. The *Discovery* had to get underway immediately or miss the tide. As the ship passed Whitehall, Hudson ordered the English flag to be raised in a salute to the king.

When the *Discovery* reached Tilbury Hope on the lower reaches of the Thames, two men came aboard. One was named Wilkinson. The other was Henry Greene. There was nothing unusual about a captain's friends or relatives meeting a ship at this spot and having a short visit before the vessel went on to the sea. But when Wilkinson went ashore at Harwich, Greene remained aboard. Thus did Hudson sneak Greene onto the *Discovery* without the knowledge of Sir Thomas Smythe and his partners.

On April 22, the *Discovery* stopped at the Isle of Sheppey in the mouth of the Thames. There, Hudson made another sudden change in the ship's roster. He sent William Coleburne back to London, with a letter explaining to the Company of Gentlemen why he had dismissed their hand-picked master's mate. Just what Hudson wrote in that letter was never revealed.

No doubt Coleburne left the ship reluctantly. With his departure, the only Company man left to monitor Hudson was Prickett, and Prickett was not a mariner. Juet, of course, was delighted to see Coleburne go, because now the position of first mate was his alone.

Once she had the freedom of the open sea, the *Discovery* made good time. The crew sighted the Orkney Islands on May 5, and the Faeroes on May 8. The *Discovery* was off the west coast of Iceland on May 11, when bad weather forced Hudson to seek the shelter of an inlet. Fog and contrary winds kept the ship on Iceland's rocky shores for three weeks, much to Hudson's dismay.

While Hudson waited impatiently for a fair wind, the crew took advantage of the unscheduled stopover. In the shadow of volcanic Mount Hekla, they enjoyed the luxury of bathing in hot springs. They hunted ducks, geese, and partridge, and feasted on the roasted birds every night.

Thomas Woodhouse, one of the few crewmen who could write, took the opportunity to compose a letter that he could send back to England with fishermen. He wrote to a friend in London about his success at bird hunting, and the pleasures of the hot springs. From the tone of Woodhouse's letter, it seemed as though the voyage was the grand adventure he'd expected it to be. But trouble and bad feelings had already begun to smolder aboard the *Discovery*.

Abacuck Prickett was a devout Christian who read his bible daily. Henry Greene took great delight in insulting Prickett's religious sensibilities. Greene also bullied Doctor Edward Wilson. One day, when the men were ashore and Hudson was not present, Greene picked a fight with Wilson over some trivial matter. Angry words quickly gave way to blows. Greene was bigger and stronger, and was an experienced street brawler. He easily beat Wilson up.

That Wilson and Greene actually fought was shocking to the crew. As ship's doctor, Wilson had the rank of an officer, and was therefore due the appropriate respect. It would have been insubordinate of Greene to so much as lay a hand on him, let alone strike him. The men were therefore outraged at Hudson's reaction when he arrived on the scene and Prickett told him about the fight.

Hudson took Greene's side, saying that "Wilson has a tongue that would wrong his best friend." He told Prickett to "let it alone."

To Wilson, this was insult added to injury. He announced that he was not getting back on the *Discovery*. He said he would stay in Iceland and go home with fishermen. Only after much pleading from the crew did Wilson finally agree to continue with the voyage. The matter should have ended there, but it did not.

Juet, whom Hudson possibly reprimanded for not stopping the fight, got drunk in his cabin. Then he told Philip Staffe that Greene was Hudson's spy below deck. In Prickett's words, Juet said Hudson had brought Greene aboard "to crack his credit that should displease him." The rumour soon spread throughout the crew.

Juet's accusation that Greene was there to tattle on the men may have been accurate. Hudson's record was checkered with shipboard uprisings. He might have considered it advantageous to have an informer who could tell him of any grumblings. His son John ate and bunked with the men, but they certainly would not let him hear any mutinous whisperings. In fact, even though John Hudson did his share of the work and was shown no favouritism by the captain, the rest of the *Discovery*'s crew never accepted him as one of them.

Whether or not Greene actually was Hudson's spy, the men now believed he was. The very idea that the ship's master would do such a thing permanently soured the relationship between captain and crew. Hudson did not learn of Juet's sedition until the ship had left Iceland, and was en route to Greenland. Staffe had summoned up the nerve to ask the captain if it was true.

Hudson was furious. He called Juet to his cabin and demanded to know if he had started such a malicious rumour. Juet defiantly admitted that he had. Hudson threatened to turn back to Iceland and put Juet ashore, leaving him to return to England with fishermen. But according to Prickett, Hudson was "otherwise persuaded." Juet was still first mate, and his opinion of Henry Hudson sank to a greater depth than ever before.

On June 9, Hudson sighted the southern tip of Greenland. He noted in his journal, "Thick ribbed ice prevented me from approaching close to the shore. I felt no regrets." The men were glad not to go ashore. They believed that Greenland was inhabited by cannibals.

Hudson took the time to chart some of the Greenland coast, to correct errors he had found on his maps. He steered clear of the "mountains of floating ice," which he had learned were but the tips of even larger masses of ice below the surface of the water. Greene and Prickett complained about the bitter cold.

Hudson set a westerly course, and on June 25, the *Discovery* sailed into the Furious Overfall. The ship was just off Resolution Island when Hudson and his men learned for themselves why the Furious Overfall had been so named.

The Furious Overfall (Hudson Strait) separates Baffin Island from the Ungava Peninsula. The currents are incredibly strong, and the tides in the strait and adjacent Ungava Bay range from five to eighteen metres. In the entire world only the tidal range of the Bay of Fundy is greater. As if the swirling currents and the mighty tides don't make the strait dangerous enough, great pans of ice come thundering down the four hundred and fifty mile long waterway, as though in a mad race to reach the Atlantic. To make matters even worse, the nearness of the North Magnetic Pole rendered compasses useless.

The shore of Baffin Island was obscured by fog when the *Discovery* entered the Furious Overfall, so Hudson did not know when he actually entered the strait. The *Discovery* was almost immediately at the mercy of the currents and tides. She was carried north, and then south again. Soon the ship was in Ungava Bay and was embayed by ice; trapped, with no visible way out!

Prickett later reported,

> Here our master was in despair and he thought
> he should never have got out of this ice, but
> there have perished. Therefore he brought forth
> his card [chart] and showed all the company,
> that he was entered above an hundred leagues
> further than any English was: and left it to their
> choice, whether they would precede any fur-
> ther; yea or nay.

Exactly what happened is not certain. The surviving pages of Hudson's journal say nothing about putting the matter of continuing the expedition to a vote. Would a man as driven to explore as Hudson have done such a thing willingly? Had the terrified crew threatened mutiny? Was Prickett's account simply a cover-up?

Juet wrote in his journal on July 26,

> A delegation came to me today to ask my opinion
> of our situation. I told them plain that Hudson
> is a fool. He hopes to reach Bantam in the East
> Indian islands by Candlemass (February 2), but
> we shall be at the bottom of the sea by then if he
> persists in his madness.

If Juet's claim was true, Hudson must have told him that he did not intend to just investigate the Furious Overfall and then return to England. The captain wanted to take the *Discovery* all the way to the Orient! This knowledge could have motivated Juet to lead a rebellion that had enough support to force Hudson into leaving the final decision up to the crew.

The men were divided. Prickett wrote, "Some were of one mind and some of another, some wishing themselves at home and some not caring where, so they were out of the ice."

In his journal, Prickett captured a moment in that argument aboard the *Discovery*. "There was one who told the master, that if he had an hundred pounds, he would give four-score and ten to be home." Prickett did not name the dissenter, but by the speaker's tone and boldness, it was probably Juet.

Then, Philip Staffe replied, "that if he had an hundred, he would not give ten upon such condition, but would think it to be as good money as ever he had any, and to bring it as well home, by the leave of God."

Staffe and the others who sided with the captain prevailed, and the *Discovery* did not turn back for England. For days the ship battled ice, wind, and the maddening currents and tides. She was carried in and out of Ungava Bay. Finally, the vessel began to make progress west. It was now the middle of the very short summer season, when the strait was free enough of ice to allow relatively clear sailing.

On August 2, the *Discovery* entered a narrow channel that seemed to be the western extremity of the strait. Hudson honoured two of his employers by naming geographic features after them; Cape Wolstenholme and Digges Islands. Fog was thick, so Hudson anchored off East Digges Island. He sent Robert Bylot, Henry Greene, Philip Staffe, and Abacuck Prickett ashore. Prickett was in charge, which suggests that Hudson did not trust Juet.

During a rainstorm the men scaled the heights of the island to see if they could get a good view of the surrounding country, but fog limited visibility. However, they spotted a herd of deer, and saw more seabirds than they had ever seen in one place before. They found stone cairns with dead birds in them; food caches of the local Natives. They also saw an abundance of sorrel, a plant with a high vitamin C content that sailors called "scurvy grass," because it cured the disease.

When the shore party heard a signal shot from the *Discovery*, they hurried back to the ship. They wanted to stay at the island for a day or two so they could hunt deer and birds, and gather sorrel. But Hudson insisted on leaving immediately. The water off the island's shore was full of shoals, and the anchorage was poor. More significantly, Hudson had noted a strong flood tide coming through the strait from the north. A flood tide could only come from a sea!

Hudson carefully guided the *Discovery* up the narrow channel. On August 3, the fog lifted, allowing Hudson to take a reading to determine his location. He wrote, "Then I observed and found the ship at 61 degrees, 20 minutes, and a sea to the westward."

That entry in Hudson's journal was the last script in his own hand that would survive for posterity. Everything that he wrote from that point on would be deliberately destroyed to cover up a major crime. A letter written by Thomas Woodhouse, which was eventually found in a desk in his cabin, described some of the subsequent events aboard the *Discovery*. But the principal eyewitness account of what happened thereafter was that of Abacuck Prickett. How much of the whole story Prickett told will never be known.

A sea to the westward! Hudson thought he had reached the Pacific Ocean. He had beaten the Furious Overfall. He had found the Northwest Passage! From the quarterdeck of the *Discovery* Hudson looked across a vast expanse of water that met the sky at the horizon. Beyond that horizon lay the Orient. Only a fool or a coward would turn back now.

Hudson sailed south into the "sea," not realizing that he was actually in a huge bay. His exact course is not known, but he eventually reached another bay at the southern extremity of his sea. His elation at finding the Northwest Passage turned to frustration as he found the way south and west blocked. Hudson refused to accept that he had reached a dead end. He sailed back and forth across what is now called James Bay, looking for a passage that did not exist.

The crew became anxious again. Hudson assured them that he knew what he was doing. He told them that they would be in the spice islands by February. Then the story reached Hudson's ears that Juet had been telling the men that the captain was lost. Hudson decided the time had come to chastise the troublesome first mate.

On September 10, Hudson summoned Juet to his cabin. He reminded Juet of the disloyalty he had shown during the crisis in Ungava Bay, and used that as an excuse to demote Juet to the level of common seaman. Robert Bylot was promoted to first mate. Juet was outraged and demanded an open hearing.

Hudson was under no obligation to grant Juet a formal hearing. But once again the captain failed to firmly assert his authority. He called the whole ship's company together to witness the proceedings. Prickett wrote that Hudson treated Juet "with all the etiquette and deference due his rank."

The hearing did not go well for Juet. He told the crew that he had seen Hudson's charts, and they showed that the *Discovery* was in completely unknown waters. He spoke mockingly of Hudson's plan to be in the East Indies by February. Then Bennett Matthew, Arnold Lodlowe, and Philip Staffe all testified that Juet had been instigating mutiny since the *Discovery* left Iceland. They said he had been telling men to keep weapons close at hand, and that at the first opportunity he would seize command and take the ship back to England. According to Matthew's testimony, Juet had said that "many would be made bloody" if anyone resisted his takeover of the ship.

The evidence against Juet was overwhelming. In other circumstances, Hudson could have put Juet ashore and left him to find his own way home. But he could not do that in an Arctic wilderness, where an abandoned man would surely perish. Hudson could have had Juet clapped in irons and confined below deck for the rest of the voyage. Instead, he merely confirmed Juet's demotion and Bylot's promotion.

The captain didn't stop there. Francis Clements, the bos'un, had been implicated in Juet's plots. Hudson demoted him to common seaman and replaced him with William Wilson. Furthermore, the officer's pay that Juet and Clements lost through their demotions would go to Bylot and Wilson, and to quartermaster John King, who had shown himself to be loyal.

For all his vile attitude, Robert Juet had taken pride in being a ship's officer. Now he was a common seaman. He'd been humiliated, and he was angry. He was not alone in his resentment toward Hudson. He had a new ally in Francis Clements. Hudson told both of them that they could redeem themselves through good behaviour, and that "he would be a means for their good, and would forget injuries." They did not believe him, so they plotted.

Meanwhile, Hudson continued to look for a southern or western exit from James Bay. He thought such a waterway might connect to the "sea" Captain John Smith had heard was somewhere to the north of Virginia. Hudson stubbornly refused to listen to his men's pleas to go back the way they had come before winter set in.

Soon after the hearing, a severe storm howled into James Bay and raged for eight days. The *Discovery* rode at anchor the whole time, and the crew was in a constant battle to keep her from foundering. On the eighth day the storm seemed to be easing up, though the seas were still heavy. Against the advice of several of the men, Hudson ordered the anchor raised. The ship was caught by huge swells before the great iron weight could be winched all the way up. Suddenly the anchor slipped free. As it plunged toward the bottom of the bay, the capstan to which it was attached by rope spun like a drill. The whirling handle struck and injured Michael Butt and Arnold Ludlowe. Fortunately, Philip Staffe was standing by with an axe. He chopped through the rope before the sinking anchor could rip the capstan right out of the ship.

Although Staffe's quick action had prevented any serious damage, the accident caused some of the men to doubt Hudson's competency. A few days later, a shore party reported seeing a human footprint in the snow that was already on the ground, though it was only early October. The thought that the land might be inhabited by "savages" unnerved the men. They wanted to go home.

But Hudson was determined to find that elusive route out of the bay that Prickett described in his journal as "a Labyrinth without end." As the captain spent weeks searching and charting the coast, the days were becoming shorter and colder. Discontent among the crew of the *Discovery* lay as thick as the grey morning mists. The crew's confidence in their captain dropped even more when he ran the ship onto a shoal, and they had to wait twelve hours for the wind and tide to free her.

By November 1, ice made escape from James Bay impossible. Hudson and his men had no choice but to spend a winter in that strange, bleak land. The *Discovery* dropped anchor in the southwestern corner of James Bay, quite likely near the mouth of the Rupert River. Hudson didn't know it, but he could hardly have chosen a worse place to spend a sub-Arctic winter. On the land side the site was sheltered from the wind by three hills, but there was no protection from the icy northern blasts that came across the bay. There were few trees nearby for firewood, so the men would have to trudge a long way through the snow to haul back fuel.

Hudson had the *Discovery* beached so the ship would not be crushed in the ice, and could be used as living quarters. He thought that he and his men were well-prepared for the winter. Because they had supplemented their supplies with fish and game during the voyage, there was still a six-month supply of food in the hold. Hudson believed that if it was well managed that should be enough to last them until spring, when they could return to Digges Islands to hunt deer and seabirds. However, he offered rewards of money for any crewmen who brought in fish or game.

Hudson thought that because their location was at a latitude even more southerly than that of England, the winter would be temperate. He did not realize that other factors besides latitude affect climate, and that winters in that part of the world are colder than any Englishman could have imagined. Nor did he realize how long it would take for the ice to go out of the bay in the spring.

A few days after the men began setting up camp, the expedition suffered its first death. John Williams, ship's gunner, died from an unknown illness. It was traditional that when a member of a crew died, his belongings were put up for auction and sold to the highest bidder, and the money turned over to the deceased's next of kin. Williams had owned a warm cloth gown that his shipmates now coveted. Everyone looked forward to bidding on it when the captain held the auction.

But the captain did not hold an auction. He gave the gown to Henry Greene. This angered the other men. Not only had Hudson broken a time-honoured tradition, he had also deprived everyone else of a chance at the warm gown.

Then Philip Staffe asked Hudson for permission to build a cabin to serve as winter quarters. He thought a cabin would be easier to heat, and would be free of the foul odours that infested the sailors' quarters in the ship. Hudson refused permission, saying that the *Discovery* would do as a shelter.

Several weeks later, Hudson changed his mind. The weather had become more severe than he had anticipated. The captain sent Bylot to tell Staffe to build a cabin. Staffe angrily refused. He said it was now too cold, with too much snow and ice, for him to build a cabin.

When Hudson learned of this he was furious. He stormed off to Staffe's quarters, dragged him out, struck him, cursed him, and threatened to hang him. The men were stunned. The captain certainly had a right to be angry if a crewman refused to obey an order, but Staffe had been one of Hudson's most loyal supporters. Juet had been guilty of far worse offences than Staffe, and had not been threatened with execution.

Staffe stood his ground. He argued that he knew what he was talking about, and Hudson didn't. Hudson still insisted that the cabin be built. Staffe relented and built a small house, though with considerable difficulty. Nobody used it. Quarters in the ship were warmer.

Hudson had given orders that the men go out hunting in pairs, never alone. Staffe was still in Hudson's bad book when he and Henry Greene went hunting together. Hudson became angry when he heard about it. When Greene and Staffe returned, Hudson took the late John Williams' warm gown from Greene and gave it to Bylot. Greene argued that the gown was his. Hudson flew into a rage. He told Greene that there would be no pay for him at the end of the voyage if he displeased the captain. According to Prickett, "The master did so rile on Greene, with so many words of disgrace, telling him, that all his friends would not trust him with twenty shillings, and therefore why should he." Hudson eventually made amends with Staffe, but Greene sided with Hudson's enemies.

An image taken from Warhafftige Relation: der dreyen newen unerhörten seltzamen Schiffart *(1598). The book was one of several based on the adventures of the crew of William Barents's 1590s voyage to the Arctic.*

For the first three months the hunting was good. The men found no large game, nor even small mammals like rabbits, but they killed hundreds of ptarmigan, as well as auks and murres, which could be clubbed or shot by the score in their rookeries. The sailors also caught plenty of fish by lowering jigging lines through holes in the ice.

In the spring, however, the birds and fish disappeared. Migrating ducks and geese settled by the thousands in the salt water marshes along the shore, but the Englishmen had no experience in hunting these waterfowl. At the approach of men or the sound of a musket shot, the birds took to wing and then settled farther off.

The first weeks of spring passed and the bay remained frozen. Hudson realized that the food supply in the *Discovery* was not going to last. The men boiled moss, and ate frogs that emerged from the mud during the slow spring melt. Men began to sicken with scurvy. Prickett was crippled with it. Doctor Wilson gave the sick men a medicinal drink he made from black spruce buds, and they soon showed signs of recovery.

The cold was a constant enemy. Men were reluctant to leave the relative warmth of the ship. When they did, they risked frostbite. But they had to go out to search for food and to bring in firewood. The men were also haunted by a deep fear of the strange land around them. They were the first Europeans to spend a winter in the North American sub-Arctic, and they had no idea of what was out there. The sailors were afraid that they were surrounded by ferocious wild animals, and most frightening of all, bloodthirsty savages!

Then one day during that spring of cold and hunger, a Native appeared; a Cree hunter. Hudson saw the man not as an enemy, but as someone who might bring them food. He approached the

Native with gifts of a knife, a mirror, and some buttons. These items were provided by King, Staffe, and Prickett. The *Discovery* was not stocked for trade, and no one else was willing to donate any of their belongings.

The man was the first Native whom the crew had seen on this voyage, and they were no doubt the first white men he had ever seen. But he evidently knew something about trade with white strangers, probably through contact with Native peoples to the south who traded with the French. He accepted the gifts, and indicated through signs that he would come back the next day.

The man did return, hauling a sled with several caribou skins, two beaver pelts, and a small amount of venison. Through signs he told Hudson that he came from a nearby village, and wanted to trade. Hudson's men needed food more than animal hides, but for some reason Hudson decided to drive a hard bargain over the caribou skins. The Native wanted to trade one skin for a hatchet. Hudson demanded two skins. The Native reluctantly agreed. Then he left, promising to come back with more pelts and more food. The Englishmen never saw him again. The venison Hudson had traded for was barely enough for one meal. Juet grumbled that the captain had been a fool to haggle over the caribou skins. Most of the men agreed that for once, Juet was right.

9

Mutiny

Gradually the ice melted away from the shoreline. The *Discovery* was still trapped, but the shallop could be used. It was in the hold in pieces, and had to be assembled by Philip Staffe. When the men saw the carpenter putting the shallop together, they had the uncomfortable suspicion that Hudson intended to resume exploring.

However, the captain sent a few men out in the shallop with a seine to see if they could net some fish. They couldn't believe their good luck. They hauled in more than five hundred fish, including trout and "a strange sea creature as large as a herring and almost as good to the taste." However, after that day the catches were small, and before long the men were again down to starvation rations.

Prickett wrote that Henry Greene and William Wilson, "with some others" plotted to steal the shallop and the seine, "and shift for themselves." The "others" probably included Juet and Clements. The situation had apparently reached the point where some of the men thought their chances of survival were better in the shallop than remaining with Hudson on the *Discovery*. They probably planned to retrace the route through the Furious Overfall, and then sail down the coast of Labrador to Newfoundland, where they could find passage back to England with fishermen. It was a hare-brained plan, which was never put into action.

Before the conspirators had an opportunity to steal the shallop, Hudson awoke one morning and saw smoke rising from land to the west across the bay. That meant Natives were nearby, perhaps the village of the man with whom he had traded. They would have food!

Taking John King and two other men, and rations for eight or nine days, Hudson set off in the shallop to try to reach the Natives. He promised to return with food. Exactly where Hudson went is not known, but it would not have been surprising if he investigated one or two river mouths in his quest for a passage out of the bay. Meanwhile, he left instructions with Bylot for the rest of the men to load the *Discovery* with firewood and fresh water, and prepare to leave.

According to Prickett, Hudson returned from his expedition to the Natives, "worse off than when he left." He had failed utterly to contact the local people. In fact, when they saw Hudson and his companions approach in their boat, the Natives set fire to the woods along the shore to prevent them from landing.

It was now June, and though there was still pack ice in the bay, Hudson felt the waters had opened enough for the *Discovery* to pass through. In a last attempt to lay in a stock of food, he sent men out to fish. After three days the catch was disappointingly small.

Before setting sail, Hudson dismissed Bylot as first mate, and replaced him with King. There was no explanation for this change. The reason might have been that King, a quartermaster, could not read navigational charts, while Bylot, an experienced mariner, could. Only the first mate had access to the captain's charts. Hudson also confiscated all navigational instruments. That meant that only he would be able to take readings and know the ship's geographic position.

The men were very suspicious that a man as unqualified as King should be made first mate, and that mariners like Juet and Bylot should be denied the use of navigational instruments. They feared that Hudson was not going to set a direct course for England, but continue his search for the Northwest Passage. After all, his "sea" had turned out to be a dead end.

On June 12, 1611, after seven-and-a-half months of being stranded at the bottom of James Bay, the *Discovery* was ready to sail. That same day, soon after getting under way, Hudson made yet another inexplicable decision. He brought out all of the remaining biscuits and cheese and had them divided up equally among the crew. Each man received one pound of biscuits and three-and-a-half pounds of cheese. The shares included equal portions of food that had spoiled. The men were told that they were now responsible for their own rationing.

This was most unusual. Other commanders in similar situations would firmly control food rationing, rather than place temptation before hungry men. The consequences were predictable. William Wilson devoured his whole biscuit supply in a day, and then fell ill with stomach cramps. Henry Greene asked another man to hold half of his biscuit rations for him, and not give it to him for a week. But within three days he was demanding that the food be given back to him.

Juet, Greene, and William Wilson whispered to other men that Hudson had a secret hoard of food that he was sharing with a few favourites like King and Staffe, and of course his son. Meanwhile, Hudson outraged the men when he told Nicholas Simms to search their sea chests for hoarded food. While there was little in the way of privacy on a seventeenth century sailing ship, a sailor's sea chest was considered inviolate. The captain had no business rummaging through a man's personal belongings. Simms found a few biscuits, but nothing more. The ill feelings of most of the crew toward Hudson had grown from resentment to hatred.

The *Discovery* sailed north from James Bay into the big bay, battling pack ice all the way. Several times the ship had to ride at anchor, waiting for a clear way through. The food supply dwindled to almost nothing, and the crew became desperate. Then they became alarmed when they realized that the ship had gradually shifted to a northwest course. Hudson wasn't sailing for England; he was going to search again for the Passage! Exasperated crewmen grumbled that the captain had gone mad.

Prickett testified later that he heard the first whispers of mutiny on the night of June 21. He was in his cabin, still bedridden from the effects of scurvy. There was a knock at the door, and two visitors crept in.

> Wilson the boatswain and Henry Greene came to me ... and told me that they and the rest of their associates would change the crew, and turn the master and all of the sick men into the shallop, letting them shift for themselves ... For three days they had not eaten anything

and were therefore resolute to either mend or end, but once begun they would go through with it or die.

When I heard this, I told them I couldn't believe what I was hearing ... that for their sakes they should not do such an evil thing in the sight of God and man, as they intended to do ... Henry Greene told me to hold my peace, saying he knew the worst, which was to be hanged when he came home; of the two choices, he would rather be hanged at home than starved abroad.

Prickett claimed that he tried to talk the conspirators out of the deed, but that only angered Greene. Prickett then asked for three days in which to convince Hudson to change his mind. The only concession he could get out of them, he said, was an agreement to wait until morning. They had been planning on seizing the ship that very night.

Soon Juet, another ringleader, came to Prickett's cabin. Prickett wrote,

[B]ecause he was an older man I thought I could reason with him; but he was worse than Henry Greene, swearing that he would justify this deed when we came home. After him came John Thomas and Michael Perce; as birds of one feather.

Prickett said that he would not participate in the mutiny, but he agreed (probably under threat) not to oppose it or to warn Hudson. He claimed that he made the mutineers swear an oath on the bible not to harm the men whom they put in the shallop. Even if true, this was thoroughly hypocritical, since the men who were being cast off were doomed.

Prickett also wrote, "Henry Greene kept the master company all night." If the statement is true, Greene cold-heartedly spent much of the night visiting Hudson in his cabin, feigning friend-ship. Most likely, Greene was there to make sure that Prickett did not warn him.

The sun rose at about 4:45 on the morning of June 22. Bennett Matthew, the cook, lured King into the hold, and then locked him in. Greene and another man engaged Staffe in conversation to keep his attention diverted while Matthew, John Thomas, and William Wilson went after Hudson. The captain opened his door when he heard a noise, and was immediately dragged to the deck and bound. Edward Wilson heard the scuffling and opened his door. He asked what was going on, and Hudson cried that he was being pinioned. The mutineers told the doctor to mind his own business if he knew what was good for him. Wilson went back into his cabin and closed the door.

Hudson demanded to know what his assailants thought they were doing. They told him he would know once he was in the shallop. While they dragged Hudson off, Juet went to get King from the hold.

Juet wanted the pleasure of taking care of King, because the former quartermaster had been given the position of first mate, which Juet felt was rightly his. However, he was unpleasantly surprised when he opened the hatch and went down into the hold. King attacked Juet with a sword he had found, and almost killed him. Juet cried out for help, and two or three other men hurried down to the hold to subdue King.

Hudson and King were tossed into the shallop, soon to be followed by John Hudson, who put up a struggle but was no match for the tough mariners who dragged him to the boat. Then the mutineers went after the sick men: Syracke Fanning, Adam Moore, and Thomas Woodhouse. Woodhouse begged the mutineers not to put him off the ship. He promised that his family would reward them if they took him back to England. His pitiful pleas fell on deaf ears. Sylvanus Bond and Francis Clement were tossed into the boat because their fingers had been ruined by frostbite, and they would be of no use in running the ship.

When John Thomas and Bennett Matthew saw that Bond and Clement were among those to be cast away, they interceded for them out of friendship. Greene, who clearly considered himself in command of the rebellion, at first refused to listen. But he finally agreed to take Bond and Clement back on the *Discovery* if two others took their place in the shallop. The unfortunate replacements were Michael Butt and Arnold Ludlowe, whose injuries — received when the anchor broke free months earlier — had never healed properly.

Finally, there was Philip Staffe. With the exception of Greene, the mutineers all wanted the carpenter to remain on the ship, because his skills would be much needed. Staffe wanted nothing to do with them. "I will not stay on this ship unless you force me to stay," he said. "Give me my tools, and may your souls be damned for all Eternity. For the love of God and master I will go down into the boat rather than accept of likelier hopes with such villains." Staffe was the only man to voluntarily leave the *Discovery*, and he took his precious tools with him.

Hudson saw Prickett looking out his cabin window, and shouted, "It is that villain Juet that has undone us!"

Prickett replied, "No, it is Greene that has done all this villainy." Prickett claimed that he pleaded once more with the mutineers. "On my knees, I besought them, for the love of God, to remember themselves, and to do as they would be done unto." It was no use.

Robert Bylot did not participate in the mutiny. Nor did he do anything to prevent it. He claimed later that he thought Hudson and those loyal to him were being put in the shallop only temporarily so that his cabin could be searched for hoarded food. He said he was not aware until it was too late that the men were being cast adrift.

The men in the boat were given some scanty provisions, and then the line connecting the shallop to the *Discovery* was cut. The mutineers took some time to ransack Hudson's cabin in search of food. Then they saw that the shallop was following the ship. The mutineers put on full sail and fled, in Prickett's words, "as from an enemy." They lost sight of the castaways. There is no record that Hudson, his son, and the seven crewmen were ever seen again.

Epilogue

Thirteen men were left aboard the *Discovery* after the mutiny. Seven made it back to England after one of the most harrowing voyages in the history of navigation: Abacuck Prickett, Robert Bylot, Edward Wilson, Francis Clements, Sylvanus Bond, Bennett Matthew, and Nicholas Simms. Of the others, William Wilson, John Thomas, Michael Perce, Adrian Motter, and Henry Greene were killed in a fight with Natives. Robert Juet died during the Atlantic crossing, and his body was unceremoniously dumped overboard.

The mutineers had kept Prickett on the ship because they believed he could present a case to the English authorities that would save their necks. Prickett was probably responsible for the removal of a large part of Hudson's journal. In Prickett's account, the mutineers did find hoarded food in Hudson's cabin. Perhaps that was true, but Prickett might have invented the story to help justify the mutiny.

Prickett was very careful to name Juet, Greene, and William Wilson, who were already dead, as the ringleaders. After a long series of hearings, the courts acquitted the survivors. Robert Bylot, who was credited with bringing the *Discovery* home, was now seen as an experienced Arctic explorer, and a valuable asset. He returned to the Arctic, but neither he nor any other explorer ever found a trace of Henry Hudson.

There were stories that the castaways made it to land, and then were killed by Natives. One version claimed that the Natives spared John Hudson and adopted him. However, there has never been any solid evidence to verify these accounts.

The fact that Hudson was betrayed by his own men has made him a tragic figure, and the mystery surrounding his death has made him a legend. The mutiny on the *Discovery* is arguably second in notoriety only to the one that took place on HMS *Bounty* in 1789, when Captain William Bligh and men loyal to him were set adrift by Fletcher Christian's mutineers. To a degree, the dramatic tale of mutiny has overshadowed the record of Hudson's accomplishments.

On his polar sea voyages, Hudson gathered geographical and other scientific information that certainly enhanced Western European knowledge of that remote part of the world. His journey up the Hudson River blazed the way for a Dutch colony that would thrive until it was lost to the English, who subsequently made it a cornerstone of a British empire in America. Nonetheless, Hudson's greatest achievement was the conquest of the Furious Overfall.

By charting that strait that mariners had held in such dread, and proving that it could be navigated, Hudson opened the door to the great inland sea of Hudson Bay. Hudson failed to find the Northwest Passage, but his final voyage of discovery gave the merchant traders of England access to the heart of Canada's fur country. Furs, especially beaver, became as valuable as Oriental spices and silks. So important was the fur trade to European economies that France and England battled for control of Hudson Bay. In a carefully orchestrated manoeuvre to monopolize the fur trade around the great bay and far into the interior, a cartel of English merchants formed the Hudson's Bay Company.

Hudson once wrote to Richard Hakluyt, "I would that my name be carved on the tablets of the sea." That dream was certainly realized. A river, a strait, and the second largest bay in the world are named after Henry Hudson. He is recognized as one of the principal pathfinders of early Canada, and has an honoured place in the gallery of Canadian heroes.

Chronology of Henry Hudson

Hudson and His Times

Canada and the World

1524
Giovanni da Verrazano explores the east coast of North America and sees the mouth of the Hudson River.

1532
Francisco Pizarro conquers the Inca Empire of Peru.

1535
Jacques Cartier explores the St. Lawrence River as far as the site of Montreal. King Henry VIII makes himself head of the English Church.

1554
English explorer Hugh Willoughby and his crew of seventy perish while searching for a Northeast Passage.

Hudson and His Times	*Canada and the World*

1555
Death of Henry Heardson
(Hudson?), a founding member of
the Muscovy Company, and possibly Henry Hudson's grandfather.

1558
Elizabeth I becomes Queen of
England.

1566
Beginning of the Dutch revolt
against Spain. Sir Humphrey
Gilbert publishes *A Discourse of
a Discoverie for a New Passage to
Cathaia.*

Ca. 1570
Henry Hudson is born, possibly
in Hertfordshire, about seventeen
miles northwest of London.

1576
English explorer Martin
Frobisher makes the first of three
attempts to find a Northwest
Passage.

1580
Francis Drake returns to England
after becoming the first English
sea captain to circumnavigate
the globe. William Bourne publishes *A Regiment for the Sea*,
which urges exploration of a
polar route to the Far East.

Hudson and His Times

1582
Richard Hakluyt publishes his first book, *Diverse Voyages Touching the Discovery of America.*

1585–88
John Davis makes three voyages into the Canadian Arctic. Possibly young Henry Hudson is present on at least one of these voyages and sees the Furious Overfall.

1588
The Spanish Armada sails against England. Henry Hudson is likely in the crew of an English ship of war when the Armada is defeated.

Canada and the World

1582
Pope Gregory XIII implements the Gregorian calendar, an improvement over the old Julian calendar.

1583
Sir Humphrey Gilbert claims Newfoundland for England.

1595
Four Dutch ships commanded by Cornelius de Houtman reach Java via the Cape of Good Hope.

1596
Dutch explorers Willem Barents and Jacob Heemskerck discover the Spitzbergen Islands and then sail on to Novaya Zemlya.

1597
Barents dies of scurvy after spending a brutal winter in

Hudson and His Times	Canada and the World
	Novaya Zemlya. Cornelius de Houtman returns to the Netherlands with only eighty-seven of the 249 men he had started out with, but the spices he brought back encourage the Dutch to send more ships east.
	1599 Samuel de Champlain first arrives in Canada. William Shakespeare and a group of actors open the Globe Theatre just outside London. On September 21, an audience sees the very first production of *Julius Caesar*. Dutch merchants selling pepper to English merchants raise the price from three shillings a pound to a larcenous eight shillings a pound.
1600 Richard Hakluyt publishes *The Principal Navigations*.	**1600** The English East India Company is founded.
1602 The Dutch East India Company (VOC) is founded.	**1602** English explorer Captain George Weymouth sails the *Discovery* one hundred leagues into the Furious Overfall before being forced back by ice.
	1603 Elizabeth I dies. King James VI of Scotland becomes James I of England.

Hudson and His Times

Canada and the World

1605
Champlain and the Sieur de Poutrincourt found Port Royal, Nova Scotia. John Davis is killed by pirates off the coast of Sumatra.

1607
April: Henry Hudson sails north in the Muscovy Company ship *Hopewell* in search of a polar route to the Far East.

June: Hudson discovers the Spitzbergen whaling grounds and claims them for England.

August: Ice forces Hudson to give up his search for a polar route to the Far East and return to England.

1607
The colony of Jamestown is founded by Captain John Smith and the Virginia Company.

1608
April: Sailing again for the Muscovy Company, Henry Hudson sets out in the *Hopewell* to find a Northeast Passage to China along the north coast of Russia.

July: Bad weather and ice prevent Hudson from finding a way through or around Novaya Zemlya. Hudson wants to sail west to explore the Furious Overfall, but his crew threatens mutiny.

1608
Champlain founds Quebec City.

Hudson and His Times	*Canada and the World*

August: Hudson returns to England and is dismissed by the Muscovy Company.

1609
January: The Dutch East India Company hires Hudson to find a Northeast Passage to the Far East

April: After many disputes with the VOC, Hudson sails from Amsterdam in the ship *Half Moon* to search for the Northeast Passage.

May: Hudson is once again blocked by ice as he approaches Novaya Zemlya. Disregarding his orders from the VOC, he turns around and sets sail for North America.

June: During the trans-Atlantic crossing, the *Half Moon* pursues a French ship, possibly for piratical purposes.

July: Hudson sails past Newfoundland and Nova Scotia. On July 18, somewhere along the New England coast Hudson first sets foot on North American soil. Hudson and his men have their first encounters with the Natives, engaging in small scale trade. A gang of sailors led by First Mate Robert Juet plunders a Native village.

Hudson and His Times

Canada and the World

August: The *Half Moon* is off the coast of the English settlement of Jamestown, Virginia. Though Hudson is a friend of Captain John Smith, he does not land because he fears a Dutch ship might not be welcomed by the English. Hudson sails as far south as Cape Hatteras, and then turns north again.

September: Hudson reaches Manhattan Island and the mouth of the Hudson River. Giovanni da Verrazano visited the river mouth in 1524, but Hudson will be the first European to explore upstream. Hudson believes the river might lead to the "seas" (Great Lakes) Captain John Smith was told about by some Natives. There are several encounters between the Europeans and the Natives, not all of them friendly. Second Mate John Colman is killed by an arrow. Hudson reaches the site of present day Albany and finds that the river above that point is not navigable. On the way downstream the *Half Moon* is attacked by Natives and several of the warriors are killed. Though Hudson has failed to find a route to the Pacific, he believes the river valley could be the site of a thriving colony.

Hudson and His Times

October: The *Half Moon* leaves the river mouth and sets sail for England, not the Netherlands.

November: The *Half Moon* docks in Dartmouth, Devonshire.

December: Hudson is arrested for working for a foreign power. He is not imprisoned, but soldiers keep him under surveillance. He is forbidden to leave England without the permission of King James I.

1610

Sir Thomas Smythe, Sir Dudley Digges, and John Wolstenholme, with the assistance of Henry the Prince of Wales, help Hudson regain the king's favour. Smythe, Digges, and Wolstenholme form an enterprise called the Company of Gentlemen and commission Hudson to search for the Northwest Passage.

April: Hudson's ship, the *Discovery*, embarks from London. On board are twenty-three people, including Captain Hudson, his son John, the troublesome Robert Juet, and Abacuk Prickett, who is most likely the representative of the Company of Gentlemen. Before the *Discovery* clears the Thames Estuary,

Canada and the World

1610

Étienne Brûlé goes to live among the Hurons and becomes the first European to see Lakes Ontario, Huron, and Superior. Galileo sees the moons of Jupiter through his newly invented telescope.

Hudson and His Times

Canada and the World

Hudson dismisses the man who has been selected as his first mate and makes Robert Juet second in command. Hudson also picks up his disreputable friend Henry Greene, whose presence aboard the ship is unknown to Smythe, Digges, and Wolstenholme.

May: The *Discovery* makes a stopover in Iceland. Already there is trouble on board. Henry Greene beats up ship's doctor Edward Wilson. Hudson later threatens to put Juet ashore in Iceland and let him return to England with the fishing fleet.

June: The *Discovery* enters the Furious Overfall (Hudson Strait) and is almost wrecked by ice in Ungava Bay. Discord is rife among the crew.

August: Hudson names Cape Wolstenholme and Digges Islands. Hudson's log ends with his entry on August 3, in which he records "a sea to the westward." The rest of his log will be destroyed by mutineers. Hudson evidently thinks he has reached the Pacific Ocean. In fact, he has discovered Hudson Bay. The only eyewitness account of the rest of the *Discovery*'s voyage will be that of Abacuk Prickett, and its truthfulness will be suspect.

Hudson and His Times

1610–11
Hudson and the crew of the *Discovery* spend a brutal winter at the bottom of James Bay. They are the first Europeans to winter in the Canadian Arctic. The men suffer from hunger, scurvy, and frostbite. According to Prickett, there are numerous disputes between Hudson and crewmen, and Hudson shows poor leadership.

June 12: James Bay is finally free enough of ice for the *Discovery* to sail. According to Prickett, the crew becomes alarmed when they realize that instead of heading home to England, Hudson intends to continue searching for the Northwest Passage.

June 22: In a mutiny led by Robert Juet and Henry Greene, Hudson, his son, and seven crewmen are put into a small boat and set adrift.

Of the thirteen men left aboard the *Discovery*, only seven will make it back to England alive. Robert Juet and Henry Greene will not be among the survivors. After a series of hearings, all of the survivors will be acquitted of charges of mutiny. There has never been any confirmed evidence that any of the castaways were ever seen again.

Canada and the World

1611
The King James Version of the Bible is published in England.

1625
The Dutch found the colony of New Amsterdam on Manhattan Island.

Bibliography

Asher, G.M. *Henry Hudson the Navigator*. London: The Hakluyt Society, 1860.

Bacon, Edgar Mayhew. *Henry Hudson: His Times and His Voyages*. New York: G.P. Putnam and Sons, 1907.

Bown, Stephen. *Merchant Kings: When Companies Ruled the World, 1600–1900*. London, U.K.: Conway Maritime Press, 2010.

Hunter, Douglas. *God's Mercies: Rivalry, Betrayal and the Dream of Discovery*. Toronto: Anchor Canada, 2008.

Hunter, Douglas. *Half Moon*. London: Bloomsbury Publishing, 2009.

Johnson, Donald S. *Charting the Sea of Darkness: The Four Voyages of Henry Hudson*. New York: Kodansha Amer Inc., 1993.

Mancall, Peter. *Fatal Journey*. New York: Basic Books, 2009.

Powys, Llewelyn. *Henry Hudson*. New York: Harper and Brothers, 1928.

Sandler, Corey. *Henry Hudson: Dreams and Obsession*. New York: Citadel Press, 2007.

Vail, Philip. *The Magnificent Adventures of Henry Hudson*. New York: Dodd, Mead and Company, 1965.

Wilson, John. *Ghosts of James Bay*. Toronto: Dundurn Press, 2009.

Wilson, John. *North with Franklin: The Lost Journals of James Fitzjames*. Markham, ON: Fitzhenry and Whiteside, 1999.

Index

Adrey, John, 55
Africa, 20, 25, 76, 78, 86, 96, 100
Albany, 142, 197
Amsterdam, 25, 79–81, 85, 87, 90,
    95–97, 100, 101, 104, 106–8, 111,
    115, 116, 119, 122, 130, 147–49,
    151–54, 196, 200
Arctic Circle, 34, 36, 120
Arctic Ocean, 21
Arkhangel'sk, 25
armaments on ships, 57, 58, 77, 120,
    121, 130, 131, 137, 145
Atlantic Ocean, 17, 21, 32, 95, 112, 116,
    117, 120, 127, 148, 168, 188, 196

Baffin Island, 22, 168
Barbary Corsairs, see pirates and
    piracy
Barents Sea, 52
Barents, William, 40, 52, 53, 83, 89,
    177, 193
Barnes, John, 56
Baxter, Thomas, 34
Bay of Fundy, 123, 168
Beuberry, James, 34
Bond, Sylvanus, 160, 186, 188
Borough, Stephen, 52
Branch, John, 55

Bristol, 27, 30, 31, 50
Brooklyn, 134
Budge Row, 24, 54, 55, 57, 85
Busse Island, 120
Butt, Michael, 160, 174, 186
Bylot, Robert, 160, 170, 172, 173, 176,
    177, 181, 182, 187, 188

Cabot, John, 16, 21
Cabot, Sebastian, 16, 80
Canada, 21, 23, 90, 122, 189, 190, 194
Cape Cod, 132
Cape Hatteras, 133, 197
Cape of Good Hope, 92, 193
Cape Wolstenholme, 170, 199
Cartier, Jacques, 21, 90, 191
Cathay, 26, 28–30, 52, 53, 84, 90, 94,
    95, see also China
Cecil, Sir Robert, 150–52
charts, 21, 28, 30, 31, 38, 39, 50, 61,
    69, 70, 73, 81, 83, 84, 88, 95, 96,
    109, 151, 152, 172, 182
Chesapeake Bay, 132
China, 13, 16, 27, 28, 31, 48, 53, 69,
    78, 98, 149, 195, see also Cathay
Clements, Francis, 160, 173, 181, 188
Coleburne, William, 161, 165
Collin, William, 33, 36, 40, 42

Colman, John, 33, 36, 39, 40, 42, 43, 46, 47, 99, 100, 105, 109, 114, 118, 129, 30, 136, 137, 197

Columbus, Christopher, 20, 80, 84

Company of Gentlemen, 158, 159, 161, 165, 198

compass, 36, 168

Cooke, John, 33, 55, 61, 66, 67

Dartmouth, England, 148–53, 198

Davis, John, 16, 17, 21, 23, 80, 193, 195

Day, Richard, 34

dead reckoning, 37

Delaware Bay, 133

De Moucheron, Balthazar, 89, 106

Digges, Sir Dudley, 155–58, 160, 163, 198, 199

Digges Islands, 170, 175, 199

discipline, 35, 86, 99, 106

Drake, Sir Francis, 18, 31, 93, 162, 192

Dutch East India Company, 76, 77, 87, 89, 103, 110, 116, 152, 194, 196

Dutch government, 49, 78, 91, 154

Dutch sailors, 100, 104, 112–14, 118, 122, 123, 131, 134, 147, 148, 152, 153

East India Company (England), 19, 97, 155, 158, 194

East India House, 82, 85–87, 89, 95, 106–9, 152

Eastern trade goods, 19, 85

Elizabeth I (Queen of England), 23, 28, 97, 154, 192, 194

England, 12–14, 16, 17, 19, 21, 23–25, 27, 28, 30, 33, 40, 44, 46, 48, 49, 53, 56, 63, 71, 74–76, 79, 80, 82, 90, 98, 105, 106, 112, 114, 122, 132, 139, 148, 150, 151, 153, 155–59, 162, 163, 166, 167, 169, 170, 173, 175, 181–83, 186, 188, 189, 192–96, 198–200

English Channel, 75

Faeroe Islands, 118, 119

falcon (small cannon), 145, 146

Fanning, Syracke, 160, 186

Far East, 19–21, 26, 42, 54, 75–77, 80, 83, 86, 192, 195, 196

fata morgana, 120

food on ships, 13, 19, 33, 68, 71, 105–6, 118, 122, 128, 129, 163, 175, 178, 181–83, 187, 188

France, 49, 76, 90, 91, 95, 122, 189

Frobisher, Martin, 21–23, 120, 192

Furious Overfall, 13, 14, 16, 17, 23, 31, 48, 71, 84, 93, 97, 98, 116, 117, 123, 146–48, 151, 152, 159, 163, 164, 168, 169, 171, 181, 189, 193–95, 199

furs, 25, 130, 131, 135, 144, 189

Geographic North Pole, 37

Gerritsz, Dirck, 100

gig, 42, 43, 46, 47, 55, 64, 136, 137, 142, 144, 145

Gilbert, Sir Humphrey, 56, 192, 193

Gilby, Humfrey, 56

Gosnold, Bartholomew, 132

grampus, 39

Gravesend, 34, 73

Great Lakes, 95, 197

Greene, Henry, 161–63, 165–68, 170, 176, 177, 180, 182–88, 199, 200

Greenland, 37–40, 48, 70, 167, 168

Gregorian calendar, 111, 112, 193

Hague, The, 83, 85, 90, 91, 93, 94, 97

Hakluyt, Richard, 17, 18, 27–31, 39, 50, 52–54, 57, 60, 63, 69, 74, 83, 84, 93, 127, 164, 190, 193, 194

Heardson, Henry (grandfather?), 16, 192

Henry IV (King of France), 90, 91, 95

Henry VIII (King of England), 26, 191

Henry, Prince of Wales, 157, 158, 198
Hilles, Thomas, 55
Hoboken, 146
Hold-with-Hope, 38
Holland, Thomas, 150, 151
Hondius, Jodocus, 93–6, 111
Hudson, Alice (granddaughter), 79
Hudson, Christopher (brother?), 16
Hudson, Henry
  as a captain and leader, 18, 32, 35,
    36, 44–46, 54–59, 67, 68, 71, 104,
    112, 113, 115, 116, 136, 137, 106–
    63, 171, 172, 173, 176, 182, 183
  as a mapmaker, 41, 58, 69, 74, 93,
    151, 168
  as a navigator, 16, 37, 71, 182
  as a pioneer of polar navigation, 16
  birth, 15
  commissioned by Muscovy
    Company, 27–31
  desire for glory over money, 18, 32,
    50, 96
  disappearance of, 187
  disgraced, 153
  early life, 16, 23
  education, 16
  family, 15, 16, 31
  first sets foot on North American
    soil, 127
  first meeting with North American
    Natives, 124–26
  hired by Dutch East India
    Company (VOC), 86–90, 96
  hired by Sir Thomas Smythe and
    the Company of Gentlemen, 158
  importance in history, 189
  journals of, 41, 48, 60–63, 70, 72, 92,
    93, 111, 120, 122, 123, 127, 128,
    135, 139–42, 144, 147, 168, 171
  obsession with finding Northwest
    Passage, 23, 48, 50, 69, 71, 79,
    108, 116, 127, 157, 171, 182, 183

personal appearance, 17
personality, 17, 127
portraits of, 17
regains royal favour, 158
served with an Order-in-Council,
  153
surveillance of, 154–58
voyages: first voyage (*Hopewell*,
  1607), 35–48
  second voyage (*Hopewell*, 1608),
    58–73
  third voyage (*Half Moon*, 1609),
    111–48
  fourth voyage (*Discovery*, 1610–
    11), 164–89
Hudson, John (son), 11, 34, 39, 65,
  96, 112, 118, 160, 167, 186, 189
Hudson, Katherine (wife), 12, 15, 31,
  32, 34, 50, 53, 79, 88, 97, 98, 151,
  162, 164
Hudson, Oliver (son), 15, 79, 97
Hudson, Richard (son), 15, 97
Hudson, Thomas (brother?), 16
Hudson Bay, 189, 199
Hudson River, 159, 189, 191, 197
Hudson Strait, 16, 168, 199
Hudson's Tutches, 48

Iceland, 118, 165–67, 172, 199
Ireland, 147, 148
Isle of Sheppey, 165
Indians, 123, 141, 144

James I (King of England), 27, 49,
  150, 194, 198
James Bay, 172–75, 182, 183, 200
Jamestown, 17, 94, 132, 195, 197
Jan Mayen Island, 48
Japan, 27, 80
Jeannin, Pierre, 91–93, 95
Juet, Robert, 56–59, 61, 63, 66–72, 99,
  100, 104, 106, 109, 111, 112, 114,

115, 117–21, 123, 124, 126, 128–
35, 137, 138, 140–46, 148, 153,
154, 158, 160–62, 165, 167, 169,
170, 172, 173, 176, 179, 181–86,
188, 196, 198–200
Julian calendar, 111, 193

Kara Sea, 52, 53, 69
Kara Strait, 52
King, John, 160, 181
Knight, James, 34

Labrador, 13, 71, 122, 123, 181
latitude, 21, 26, 37, 175
Le Maire, Isaac, 87, 88–91, 103
Le Maire, Jacob, 91–93, 95
lie-a-trie, 121
Limehouse, 56
Lofoten Islands, 58, 71, 117
London, England, 12, 16, 20, 24, 25,
29, 31, 33, 34, 56, 63, 72, 78, 79,
82, 85, 88, 89, 93, 94, 98, 106, 150,
153–55, 158, 161, 165, 166, 195,
194, 198
longitude, 37
Ludlowe, Arnold, 55, 63, 174, 186

Maine, 123
Magellan, Ferdinand, 21, 92
Magnetic North Pole, 37
Manhattan Island, 136, 197, 200
maps, 21, 69, 74, 93–95, 151, 168
Matochkin Strait, 52, 53, 69
Matthew, Bennett, 160, 172, 173, 185,
186, 188
Mediterranean Sea, 17
mermaids, 60
Mohawks, 143
Moore, Adam, 160, 186
morses, *see* walrus
Mount Hekla, 166
Muscovy Company, 16, 19, 24–30,

32–34, 38, 42, 44, 49, 50, 53–57,
61, 69, 73, 74, 76–78, 81, 85, 87, 91,
97, 150, 158, 192, 195, 196
mutineers, 12, 13, 72, 116, 147,
185–89, 199
mutiny, 12, 48, 72, 73, 115, 116, 123,
148, 169, 172, 183, 184, 187–89,
200

Narrows, the, 136
narwhal, 53
Natives (North American), 13, 94, 95,
125, 126, 128–32, 134–41, 143–45,
171, 181, 188, 189, 196, 197
Netherlands, 49, 76, 83, 97, 98, 104,
111, 116, 194, 198
New Holland, 132
New World, 20, 75, 76, 78, 84, 116, 127,
128, 132, 138, 139, 144, 151, 158
Newfoundland, 13, 16, 21, 26, 122,
146, 147, 151, 181, 193, 196
Newland, 40
North America, 21, 71, 95, 127, 178,
191, 196
North Cape, 59, 113
North Pole, 26, 27, 37, 38, 40, 44, 48,
50, 93
Northeast Passage, 25, 29, 42, 50, 52,
54, 61, 69, 70, 72, 73, 78–80, 84,
87–89, 93, 94, 96, 97, 107–9, 115,
128, 191, 195, 196
Northwest Passage, 14, 16, 17, 21, 25,
29, 48, 71, 72, 74, 82, 84, 90, 91,
93–95, 97, 102, 116, 147, 152, 155,
157–59, 163, 164, 171, 172, 182,
189, 192, 198, 200
Norway, 25, 49, 58, 59, 71, 113
Norwegian Sea, 118
Nova Scotia, 122, 123, 195, 196
Novaya Zemlya, 50, 52, 53, 56, 61,
63, 69–71, 73, 96, 113, 115, 117,
193–96

Ob River, 53
Order-in-Council, 153–55, 157
Orkney Islands, 165
Orient, 19, 53, 58, 78, 79, 86, 87, 93, 96, 127, 163, 169, 171, 189

Pacific Ocean, 13, 21, 58, 94, 95, 98, 133, 134, 142, 146, 152, 171, 197, 199
pack ice, 27, 44, 181, 183
Palisades, 139
Penobscot Bay, 123
Perce, Michael, 55, 160, 184, 188
Pet Strait, 52
Philip II (King of Spain), 75
pirates and piracy, 17, 20, 28, 32, 555, 58, 72, 76, 80, 93, 94, 117, 121, 131, 147, 150, 181, 195, 196
Plancius, Peter, 52, 83–85, 88, 90–95, 97, 98, 101, 106, 107, 111, 127
Playse, John, 34
Polar Seas, 107, 115
Poppe, Jan, 87, 89, 90, 96
Portugal, 20, 21, 32, 49, 75, 76
Prickett, Abacuck, 160, 161, 165–72, 174, 177–81, 183–88, 198–200
Purchas, Samuel, 31, 74

Raleigh, Sir Walter, 154, 157
rats, 32, 105
Raynor, Robert, 55
Resolution Island, 168
Rupert River, 175
Russia, 25, 50, 52, 53, 58, 70, 84, 149, 155, 195

St. Ethelburga's Church, 34
St. George River, 127
St. Lawrence River, 13, 21, 90, 116
Salee Rovers, *see* pirates and piracy
Sandy Hook, 133, 137
Schenectadea, 143

Scotland, 34, 56, 76, 118, 151, 194
scurvy, 21, 150, 171, 178, 183, 193, 200
sea anchor, 40, 119
sea-beggars, 100
seals, 41, 42, 49, 60, 61, 119
Severny Island, 52
shallop, 11–13, 55, 59, 64, 66–68, 163, 180, 181, 183, 185–87
Shetland Islands, 34
shoal, 66, 67, 124, 134, 171, 174
ships
    Discovery, 12–14, 159–72, 174–76, 178–83, 186–89, 194, 198–200
    Half Moon, 102–4, 106–28, 130–36, 138, 139, 142–53, 159, 196–98
    Hopewell, 32–4, 38–41, 43–8, 53–9, 64, 66–8, 70, 71, 73, 159, 195
    living conditions on, 32–34, 36, 105
Simms, Nicholas, 160, 183, 188
Skrutton, James, 34, 55
slake, 114, 115
Smith, Captain John, 17, 18, 27, 94, 95, 116, 117, 123, 132–34, 147, 173, 195, 197
Smythe, Sir Thomas, 17, 18, 155, 157–59, 161, 163–65, 198, 199
solar halo, 115
Spain, 17, 20, 21, 24, 42, 75, 76, 78, 92, 192
Spanish Armada, 16, 17, 24, 75, 193
spies, 25, 28, 49, 78, 103, 107, 109
Spitzbergen Islands, 40, 44, 45, 49, 50, 73, 156, 193
Staffe, Philip, 56, 58, 59, 63, 160, 167, 170, 172, 174, 176, 177, 179, 180, 183, 185, 186
Staten Island, 134
Stromo Island, 119
sunspot, 114, 115
superstitions, 35, 39, 115, 133

Thames (River and Estuary), 25, 48, 165, 198
Thomas, John, 160, 184–86, 188
Thorne, Robert, 25–27, 38
Tilbury, 48, 165
Tomson, Richard, 55
Tower of London, 15, 154

Ungava Bay, 168, 170, 172, 199
Ungava Peninsula, 168
unicorns, 53, 60

VOC (*De Vereenigde Oost-Indische Compagnie*), 77, 78, 80–91, 95–97, 99–104, 106–11, 115, 116, 122, 128, 132, 152, 154, 194, 196
Vaigach Island, 52
van Heemskerk, Jacob, 83
Van Meteran, Emanuel, 78, 79, 88, 154, 155
Van Os, Dirk, 83, 87, 89, 90, 96, 103–9
Venice, 19
Verrazano, Giovanni da, 134, 191, 197
Virginia, 17, 27, 28, 94, 116, 132, 152, 173, 195, 197

Walrus, 43, 49, 56, 63–65, 73
West Indies, 20
Weymouth, George, 97, 98, 159, 161, 194
whales and whaling, 39, 41–44, 49, 50, 63, 73, 99, 156, 195
Whale Bay, 42, 44, 54, 61
whipstaff, 46, 32, 40
White Sea, 25
Whitehall, 154, 158, 165
Williams, John, 160, 175–77
Willoughby, Sir Hugh, 52, 191
Wilson, Edward, 160, 166, 167, 178, 185, 199
Wilson, William, 160, 173, 180, 182, 183, 185, 188
Woodhouse, Thomas, 160, 166, 171, 186

Young, James, 33, 36, 40
Yuzhny Island, 52

Zeeland, 100, 101
Zielverkoopers, 86, 87
Zuider Zee, 80, 112

Marquis Book Printing Inc.

Québec, Canada
2009